The Change²

Insights into Self-Empowerment
Jim Lutes ~ Jim Britt

With

Co-authors

Co-authors

Misty Anderson

Shannon Graham

Lindsay Hallead

Tamara Renee

Yogini

Antonetta Fernandes

Christa Bonnet

Mavis Mazhura Ureke

Stacey Cargnelutti

Ellie K. Borden

Darcey Pollard

Stephanie Gamble

Georgina Elliott

Caroline Gregory Pen

Andrea Isaacs

Chiwa Higashi

Tina Sanchoo

Ashley Dais

Jan Haldane

Sarah Jean Aguinaldo

The Change²

Jim Britt ~ Jim Lutes

All Rights Reserved

Copyright 2014

The Change

10556 Combie Road, Suite 6205

Auburn, CA. 95602

The use of any part of this publication reproduced, stored in any retrieval system, or transmitted in any forms or by any means, electronic or otherwise, without the prior written consent of the publisher is an infringement of copyright law.

Jim Lutes ~ Jim Britt

The Change

ISBN 978-0-692-35729-3 (paperback)

ISBN 978-0-692-35730-9 (Amazon Kindle)

The Change is proud to support Good Women International

Every 5 minutes one American child (many as young as 10 years old) will be abducted and trafficked into the sex trade. 274 children a day. 100,000 each year and that estimate could be low. The total current number of human trafficking victims in the U.S. alone reaches into the hundreds of thousands and world-wide into the millions.

All profits from the sale of Amazon Kindle electronic books 1 through 4 are being donated to Good Women International, whose focus is on prevention of sexual exploitation of young women and children. They support self-empowerment and educational programs world-wide designed to educate our youth to avoid becoming a victim. A recent successful project was an anti-trafficking curricula for our high schools which is now complete.

Enslavement is a reality. It is documented and it is real. The question is: What are we going to do about it?

To make a donation to Good Women International, a non-profit corporation, go to: www.SupportGoodWomen.com All donations are tax deductable.

Note: *Donations never for salaries, as Good Women is a volunteer organization*

Insights into Self-Empowerment

DEDICATION

This book is dedicated to all those seeking change

The Change 2

Foreword

Berny Dohrmann, Chairman of CEO Space International

To The Readers of *The Change* Series

Jim Britt has been a mentor to *Chicken Soup* authors, and to some of the leading thought leaders on earth. Jim Britt's ground breaking work in *Letting Go*, releasing past trauma's and betrayals in life to return once again to forward looking manifestation within your full powers, has been instructed at leading *Fortune* companies and to standing room only seminars all over the world. For three decades, Jim Britt has been the "trainer of the trainers," of which I am only one. Jim has been an instructor at CEO Space, the most prestigious, hard to get into faculty on the planet, where he developed millions of dollars of resources as he assisted others to develop tens of millions of dollars for their own dream making. Jim is the most "unchanged by success and wealth" man I have ever known. He is an unselfish archangel, like in his book *Rings of Truth*.

Today, Jim Britt and Jim Lutes, along with many inspiring co-authors from around the world, bring a pioneering work to the market to transform your own journey into master manifestation. Their principles are forged on coaching millions on every continent. As you read, you are exploring self-development as the world has yet to practice. In fact, Jim and Jim's publications lead to this one APEX MOMENT. Everything you have done to date in your own life, everyone you have met, every lesson you have learned, has led you to this one GREAT life opportunity… the moment of your own transformation into ever rising full potentials.

The Change 2

As a five time best selling author myself, as a film maker, and with CEO Space, you can imagine how fussy I am to write a forward to publications in the self-development space. CEO Space was just ranked by *Forbes Magazine* as the leading entrepreneur firm, which hosts five annual business growth conferences serving over 140 countries. It was also named as THE MEETING in the world that YOU CAN NOT AFFORD TO MISS, also by *Forbes*. The world today demands more than a reputation defender to secure your forward brand, it requires that you take responsibility for your own brand and reputation in life. This book will inspire you to do just that.

CEO Space International has supported launches for many amazing works including *Chicken Soup for the Soul*, *Men Are From Mars, Women Are From Venus*, *Rich Dad, Poor Dad*, *The Secret*, *No Matter What*, *Three Feet From Gold*, *Conversations With The King*, and now the movies *Growing Up Graceland* and *Wish Man* (for Make a Wish Foundation), *Outwitting the Devil* by Napoleon Hill and Sharon Lechter, Tony Robbins' great publications, of course Jim Britt's best-selling book *Rings of Truth*; and so many more. The totals have reached more than 2 billion eye balls! You can't play around with that Mount Everest of credibility that I guard like a bank vault!

You can therefore appreciate why I encourage 100% of our followers of all the publications named, to BUY JIM BRITT and JIM LUTES book series *The Change* as a customer recognition for your own ten best close relationships or clients. But don't just buy this book, rather I endorse that you buy 10, and you gift wrap them to acknowledge your most important top ten relationships in life, or clients in business. By doing so you will retain more clients and encourage repeat buying. You may also receive more referrals and strengthen each relationship. The laws of giving will come back to you 10 to 1. When you give freely, you will always receive a rain into your life just as you rain into the lives of those you treasure. Jim Britt, Jim Lutes, and the insightful and inspiring co-authors have given you in *The Change* series, a great opportunity... more important than pouring ice water over someone's head on YouTube as a challenge for charity! The gift that keeps on giving begins when you step up and BUY 10, knowing you have been instrumental in inspiring 10 friends to live a better life. Together we are going to reach 1 BILLION SOULS as we help Jim Britt, Jim Lutes, and their co-authors to achieve their goal to transform human consciousness in our lifetime. Like Zig Ziglar, Jim Rohn, the great Roger Anthony, and so many friends who have passed, my friend Jim Britt is now an historical event in every training, every publication, and every online work at CEO Space. If you ever have the opportunity, STOP YOUR LIFE and see JIM BRITT & JIM LUTES LIVE and you will thank me personally, I know.

Their work is powerful. You'll let go of the baggage you been carrying around for years and learn to embrace everything that creates the future you want and deserve. As you close the pages of any of *The Change* books, you will say over and over again "THANK YOU Jim Britt and Jim Lutes for creating this work." You will gain a new life of super focus as never before and you will commence to master manifest in your own individual life as never before. *The Change* books provide tools to transform results for corporations, institutions and individuals, and once applied it will be impossible to miss your future success in life.

In my opinion, there are only the following areas to embrace for each of us:

- Spiritual oneness and balance
- Recreational balance and nature
- Relationship where *Perfection Can Be Had!* (my book)
  - Career attainment of goals you, yourself reset along the way

- Parenting either directly or by embracing a child you adopt to mentor at any and every age in life

These perspectives come into alignment within a framework of Jim Britt and Jim Lutes imagination along with decades of human-potential work. My advice is this work is a "BUY 10 TO SHARE WITH FRIENDS" pledge. In fact, a billion readers is a global path that Jim Britt and Jim Lutes are going to achieve NEXT for the world common good.

Let's help in this quest, as both men unselfishly donate their only asset, their precious LIFE TIME, to elevate one life at a time to their full potential and greatness.

My final request to all those who are reading my forward is that you DO IT NOW. When you think of the good you will be doing, just ask yourself, "How long will I make them WAIT?"

I'm buying my 10 today!

Berny Dohrmann

Chairman, CEO Space International

P.S. I so approve this message for all my readers and followers worldwide. CEO Space has helped authors break the book of all records a half a dozen times, which means the only record to beat can be done with the publication you are buying 10 of now. Together we are going to set a global record with one publication. Make the PLEDGE and give the gift of personal development. DO IT TODAY!

Table of Contents

Foreword vii
    JIM BRITT

Resolving Conflict in Relationships 2
    Jim Lutes

The Power of Emotional Expectation 11
    Tina Sanchoo

The Power of Surrender 22
    Andrea Isaacs

Body Wisdom: 34
    Antonetta Fernandes

A Voice Awakened 46
    Ellie K. Borden

CHOICE: It's Much More Powerful Than You May Think. *It's the KEY.* 56
    Ashley Dais

Understanding and Healing Emotional Pain 68

Caroline Gregory Pen 77

Discover the Ultimate Formulae to Get what you want, the Easy way: Victory Vibes, you're ready for them, aren't you? 78

Christa Bonnet

Empower Yourself On The Journey Of Collaboration From 'Me' To 'We' 90

Georgina Elliott

The Summit of Change 102

Jan Haldane

If I Can Heal My Heart, So Can You 114

Lindsay J. Hallead

When to Say Yes, How to Say No 126

Chiwa Higashi

My Journey Into The Heart 140

Mavis Mazhura, MA

From Awareness to Transformation 152

Misty Anderson

Pre-destiny or Choice 164

Sarah Jean Aguinaldo

Consciousness Is The Catalyst For Change 178

Shannon Graham

Visionary Leadership 192

Stephanie Ann Gamble

Build your mind, reframe your thoughts, and live your most excellent life!... 204
   Yogini

Coming Home.. 216
   Stacey Cargnelutti

From Faith to Fitness 227
   Darcey Pollard

Achieving Connection Through Disconnecting............................... 240
   Tamara Renee

Your Food-Truth.. 252

Afterword... 275

The Change 2

JIM BRITT

Jim Britt is an internationally recognized leader in the field of peak performance and personal empowerment training. He is author of 13 best-selling books including, *Cracking the Rich Code, Cracking the Life Code, Rings of Truth, The Power of Letting Go, Freedom, Unleashing Your Authentic Power, Do This. Get Rich-For Entrepreneurs, The Flaw in The Law of Attraction* and *The Law of Realization*, to name a few.

Jim has presented seminars throughout the world sharing his success principles and life enhancing realizations with thousands of audiences, totaling over 1,000,000 people from all walks of life.

Jim has served as a success counselor to over 300 corporations worldwide. He was recently named as one of the world's top 20 success coaches and presented with the best of the best award out of the top 100 contributors of all time to the direct selling industry. He also mentored/coached Anthony Robbins for his first five years in business.

Jim is more than aware of the challenges we all face in making adaptive changes for a sustainable future.

Resolving Conflict in Relationships

By Jim Britt

Are you tired of experiencing conflict in your relationships? Do you ever find yourself choosing the wrong person repeatedly? Have you ever thought, "if only I'd known…" about my partner? Do you find yourself in conflict with a co-worker? Have you ever had conflict with a parent or sibling that you can't seem to resolve?

Life is about relationships and they come in many different forms, from personal and family, to work and Leisure. Anytime you are in the presence on another person, you are in a relationship with that person. When you are with another person you are "relating" to that person.

Just imagine what it would be like if you could have a relationship where you could easily resolve problem, make conscious choices, feel comfortable and you both felt fully empowered. Imagine being able to let go of potentially destructive negative emotional patterns that are causing you conflict in your relationships.

When we find ourselves struggling in a relationship or wondering whether we will ever find that "right" someone with whom to share our lives, or handling that office conflict with a co-worker, resolving the problem sometimes seems almost impossible, doesn't it?

We were all born loving and lovable and with our own unique qualities. Our true essence is love, joy and happiness. However, as we grow older, significant people in our lives tell us through their language and behaviors, that we are not okay. As we have less than positive experiences, we internalize them. These experiences surface later in life in the form of feelings, emotions, beliefs and behavior patterns. Many of these experiences cause us to develop a distorted view of ourselves, covering up our true essence and blinding us to our loving qualities. In other words, we develop distorted beliefs about who we are. And then we unconsciously defend those very beliefs as true, even though they are what's causing us conflict. Because it is so painful, and even sometimes shameful, we put up a "socially acceptable" front built around our need to be accepted or our need to stay in control. These two needs are at the root of all our problems, both in relationships and other areas of our lives as well.

As an example, let's say a child has a need for a hug, and the parent, unknowingly, ignores the child's need. As a result, the child then develops loud behaviors in order to gain attention. Annoyed by the child's behavior, the parent then yells angrily at the child and sends him to his room. The child now feels even more rejected. The child loves and trusts his parents and counts on them for his survival. He assumes that they can't be wrong because they are the authority he looks up to for guidance. The child's conclusion is this: "It's my fault. There must be something wrong with me, otherwise I wouldn't feel this way." The child then ends up being critical of himself for feeling the way he does, but at the same time he feels he has to feel that way in order to survive. The end result is, Self-criticism = His Survival; and the other way around, His Survival = Self-criticism.

The child then decides to be perfect in order to gain the love he so desperately wants. Then a sort of "sub-personality" is born. Let's call it "The judge." The judge determines "right" from "wrong." Over time, in his effort to be "right," he overcompensates trying to be perfect and eventually nothing about him is good enough. His conclusion becomes as follows: "Needs are bad." "I'm bad for having needs." "I hate myself for not being good enough." "I don't deserve happiness." "It's all my fault, so there must be something wrong with me."

Later in life, these self-criticism patterns show up as emotional reactions - fear, anger, depression, loneliness, anxiety, perfectionism and addictions - which result in the behavior patterns of the "need for acceptance" or the "need to be in control."

In relationships where one person has an extreme need for acceptance and the other has an extreme need for control, most often they'll end up in constant conflict or even an abusive situation. Even one's need for control is really the person's deeper need for acceptance. Their behavior just shows up as needing to be the controller. Either way, if these issues aren't dealt with, the relationship is doomed for failure. When we interact with another from either of these behaviors, we do not connect from a place of whom we really are, our resourceful loving nature. We then lose our ability to see the truth in the situation and are not open to the correct solutions. When we let go of our need for approval, we can then communicate with an open heart from a place of love. And only then can you have a conflict-free relationship.

The need to be loved, approved of, to have a connection with another, is the greatest of all human needs. As a child, we feel the need to be accepted, loved and connected to our parents. That need is so strong that we carry it with us all our lives. As we grow into childhood and teen years, we feel a need to be accepted by our peers. Our friendship circles are made up of people who satisfy our need to be accepted. As we begin to form significant relationships, the need for acceptance plays a major role in the people who are attracted to us. We look for acceptance from those with whom we work. When we marry, we have a need to be accepted by our spouse. And when we become parents ourselves, we want to be accepted by our children. When they grow older and become adults, we want them to love us and remain connected. And as grandparents, we want to be accepted by the grand children, and so on.

Our greatest problem lies in the need. A "need" is defined as "a situation of great difficulty or misfortune." When we are in a state of "need" for anything, we are automatically in a state of difficulty. Need has the same meaning as lack. Lack is defined as "the state of being without or not having enough of something." When we focus on our "need for acceptance," we are focused on lack, and with that we will always find ourselves in a state of need or lack of acceptance. So, when we "need" acceptance it means we have none. When you let go of your need for acceptance, you find that others are accepting of you, as well as you are more accepting of others.

People who have a deep "need" for acceptance from others are like vacuum cleaners sucking up attention. Of course, it varies in degree, but when it's there, these people are often very tiring to be around. They are almost impossible to accept when they are so needy of validation and aren't accepting of themselves. People seeking acceptance from the outside world can't receive it until their inside world "feels" it. It can be a vicious endless cycle, especially if you don't know you are in this cycle, or how to break free.

Being in any sort of relationship - personal, business or otherwise - with someone who has a need to be accepted, is a "no win" situation. They want to please you. And if you try to please them it puts you in the cycle of now being the pleaser, but you can never really please them. No matter what you do or how hard you try, you can never really please them or fulfill their needs. This creates frustration, blame and judgment, all of which create very unfulfilling relationships. In order for someone to be pleased, they must first be pleasing to, and accept themselves.

There are basically two human emotions, "love" and "fear." I lump all negative emotions like anger, sadness, anxiety, etc., into fear. For example, anger is a fear of not being right. Sadness is a fear of losing someone or something. And anxiety is three emotions - fear, anger and depression - all mixed into one. The fear holds you back. The anger pushes you forward. The depression holds you inward. When you experience anxiety, you are going in three different directions at one time. You feel that you need to speed up, when in reality, you need to slow down and re-group. Any feeling of fear is the supporting mechanism behind our need for acceptance. Fear is simply taking a past experience, projecting it into the future with the anticipation of it happening again, and then re-living it in the present. It's a made up story. It's not real unless you make it so.

Fear restricts our energy and holds us back. Fear usually comes from not wanting to repeat the same mistake again. So many people go into the next relationship not wanting to repeat the same mistake again. And yet, they often find themselves repeating it again. So, approach every relationship with an open mind and open heart. Fear can be anything that is not loving. We may experience our fear as loneliness, resentment from a past relationship, or being stuck and feeling there is no way out. We may express our fear as sadness when we have to live without something or someone we have lost. When we are in a state of anger, we fear what we may lose or we fear not being heard, or being right. All of which stem from our need for acceptance.

It is really quite simple. When you let go of the "need for acceptance," you'll gain the acceptance of others. When you let go, you gain true power and accept yourself. When you let go of a fear, or the need for acceptance, you inherit the freedom of the present moment - a freedom to choose and act from a place of certainty, confidence and love. When you free up your mental, emotional and physical energy that has been bound up by your needs, your actions surrounding events - and your perception of those events - take on an effortless almost magical quality... a flow.

Everyone wants to love and be loved. When we truly love and accept ourselves as we let go of need to "be" accepted, only then are we free to fully love, be loved and accept others unconditionally. When "we" change, those around us change. When "we" become more loving toward ourselves, those around us become more loving toward us.

In order to resolve conflicts, make the right choice, or "be" the right choice in a relationship. It is essential to understand these dynamics. When we are stuck in our problems, conflicts and needs, we are not free to see creative options or to make healthy choices.

In order to experience a joyous relationship, two things are necessary. One, is self-observation. Self-observation is not the same as self-awareness. You can be aware that you are experiencing conflict, anger, fear, etc. Self-awareness is of little value when it comes to changing. Self-observation, on the other hand, is backing away from the conflict and viewing it from a higher perspective. In other words, separate yourself from the conflict and look for the real truth behind the conflict. What are you contributing to the conflict? Is it my need for acceptance or control? As a preventive measure, on occasion ask yourself, "what's it like being in a relationship with a person like me?" And then listen for the truth!

Through this simple process of self-observation and taking responsibility, you will very quickly begin to see what you bring to the relationship, what issues needs to be resolved, as well as how to resolve them. When we are always looking outside of ourselves or to the other person for the answers, or we place blame, we are always focused on the "perceived" problem, instead of taking responsibility for our own actions and being open to solutions. By becoming more self-observant, we can see the truth behind our fears and conflicts, let them go and move past them.

The second thing that is necessary in order to have a successful relationship is building upon our own qualities - acknowledging your talents, strengths, successes, values and goals. We should all take time out to acknowledge our strengths.

When we build more upon our strengths, acknowledge and let go of our fears, only then are we free to live our lives in the present moment… which is where real life and real love exists! By living fully in the present, we develop the freedom to choose and act from a place of clarity, love and confidence.

To Contact Jim:

www.JimBritt.com
www.PowerOfLettingGo.com
www.JourneyBeginsNow.com
www.Facebook.com/JimBrittOnline
www.linkedin.com/pub/jim-britt/5/810/245

To schedule Jim Britt as a speaker for your next special event email Support@JimBritt.com

Jim Lutes

Say the name Jim Lutes and chances are a top performer in your company has attended one or more of his dynamic trainings over the last few years.

Having taught his branded form of human performance since the early 1990s, Mr. Lutes has accelerated top level entrepreneurs throughout his career by conducting trainings on personal growth and subconscious programming into worldwide markets.

During this time Jim took his skills regarding the human mind, and combining it with trainings on influence, persuasion and communication strategies, he launched Lutes International in the early 1990s. Based in San Diego California, Jim has taught seminars for corporations, sales forces, individuals and athletes. Having appeared on television, radio and worldwide stages, Jim's style, knowledge and effectiveness provide profound results.

"Jim Lutes possesses a unique ability to create performance change in an individual in a fraction of the time it takes his competitors." The core of humans decisions are based on the programs we acquire, reinforce and grow. Combining Jim's various trainings, individuals can reach new levels of achievement and fulfillment in all areas of life. The results are at times nothing short of astonishing.

"My goal is to take that embryonic greatness that exists inside every person in America, foster it, empower it, and then hand them personal strategies based on solid principles that allow them to take that new attitude and apply it to creating a life by design."

The Power of Emotional Expectation

By Jim Lutes

At some point, you will begin to see in your own life how your thoughts create your reality. You may be more aware of the Universal Laws and see them in action in your daily life, too. You may have started using the techniques for adjusting your mind. Have you started noticing your emotions, however? I want to really dive deep into just how powerful emotional expectation is when trying to reprogram your subconscious.

The power of expectation is tremendous. Most of you may be aware of the work of Ivan Pavlov, Nobel Laureate in 1904. Pavlov studied digestive processes of animals, and his work became famously known after he observed dog's salivating at the sound of a buzzer that went off when food was given to them. The dogs knew that food was related to the sound of the buzzer – they had the expectation that they would be fed, and thus salivated.

We are not that much different than Pavlov's dogs when it comes to expectation and response. It has been proven that when we are engaged in expecting good things, our dopamine levels rise. When we have an expectation that is unmet, our dopamine lowers, and the disappointment felt can sometimes be quite strong. We are motivated to expect greater things in life and it is possible that the expecting part is the best part.

Along with these observations comes another observation, wherein, what is expected comes to be. Slightly less grounded in science than our other perceptions of expectation, this rule is loosely based around the Law of Attraction, which claims that like attracts like. What we expect, we receive. This is true all around us, whether we are using this for the purposes of manifesting our lives, or are not even aware of it.

Take as another example, how we treat each other as humans. How many different beliefs and stereotypes affect our expectations of each other every day, without our even being aware of it? Think of the bad kid in school – always misbehaving, getting into trouble. What happened to that kid? His teachers expected he would misbehave and get into trouble. So, he misbehaved and got into trouble. It is a never ending cycle that perpetuates itself.

We have expectations all the time, about everything, from how the day should look to expecting our partners to be home on time for dinner. We have expectations of others and ourselves, expectations about how to show up with each other, or of what we are really capable.

This is all part of the big E - expectation; expectation in a general sense. What I really want to focus on is the power of emotional expectation in creating your life masterpiece. We go through life with expectations of ourselves and others, or of the things we want to do, or how we want to live… and we don't pay nearly enough attention to the power these expectations really have. When you have an expectation coupled with a strong emotion, you are creating that expectation in your experience of reality. This is powerful stuff!

The rule of the mind that states, "What is expected comes to be realized." When you really integrate this concept, you will start to really pay close attention to what you say, what you think, what expectations you hold for yourself and others in terms of behavior. When you really understand the power that the mind and emotion working together yield for you, with the right action, things can start to change – and quickly – in your life.

How do you talk to yourself in the day? Let's say you are up for a big promotion at work – how do you prepare yourself on the morning you are due to hear the news? Do you look in the mirror, hopeless, and tell yourself you won't get it? Or do you look in the mirror with full knowing that the promotion is yours… and tell your reflection the same? If you expect to be passed by for this promotion, you will be. And you will continue to be, until you recognize that your expectation is creating your reality.

What if you are in a relationship that suddenly heads towards the finish line? Did you expect that relationship to go awry? Sure, sometimes we really are blindsided by life and what it hands us. Most of the time, however, we have expectations hiding in our subconscious minds that express themselves through our reality.

What is happening with your thoughts, and your inner dialogue, is that you are putting orders into the subconscious mind with each thought. The subconscious mind cannot differentiate between reality and imagination, and it wants to provide you with what you want. So if you want good health, you cannot go around thinking or saying "I'm sick" all the time. Think about times you do this in your life. It is incredibly common among so many people to walk around all day thinking either, "I'm so broke," "I'm so tired," or any other limiting thought. Until you really start paying attention to the thoughts that affect you the most, you are running stories out of your subconscious that you are probably not even aware of!

I have an exercise I like to do in my seminars, where I will invite a participant onto the stage and ask him or her to repeat after me. Then the phrase I give them is usually along the lines of: "I have a fatal disease." Nine times out of ten, no one wants to repeat this phrase. Why? Because they know - or at least, they may have just learned that night - that what they expect becomes reality. Saying "I have a fatal disease" is scary, because it tells your subconscious you have a fatal disease, and you worry you might contract a fatal disease. What these people don't realize, however, is that they leave my seminar and head home for the evening... all the while telling themselves they are broke, they are going to be single forever, they are not lovable, they are tired, they feel unwell... you name it! You have to get clear on what you are thinking and what thoughts and messages are going to your subconscious mind, it's that simple.

It is that simple, yes, but it still takes a lot of work. It requires diligence and awareness to stay on top of your thoughts. Of course, you can't possibly gauge every single thought that comes through your mind, but you can at least detect the habitual thoughts and thought patterns that are like your old friends. You must know what those are. Do you have a refrain you repeat daily without thinking about it? Look around you - how you are living right now is a good indication of how you are thinking. Are your finances in order? Are you wealthy or just getting by? Is your relationship healthy? Is your body healthy? How do you respond when emotions get hold of you? Are you resilient?

It's not enough to dream about a big yacht and think that it will simply come to you. If you believe that, you may need to go back to chapter one and read again all of the concepts we have discussed so far. It is the awareness of what you are thinking, catching yourself in the act of thinking, and replacing those thoughts with what you really want. That is the work required. Yes – it's work. Backup thought replacement with emotion, and then you will begin to see the changes you wish to see in your life.

The subconscious thinks in images and cannot hear a negative. So, let that inform your first foray into redirecting your thoughts to the positive. For example, if I tell you not to think of an elephant, chances are you thought of the elephant. When you are thinking about what you want, or expecting what you want, you cannot phrase it as: "I don't want ___." You must phrase the thought in the affirmative so that the subconscious receives a very clear message. Your current thought patterns are deeply entrenched within your neural networks, and they only continue to be reinforced when you repeat them again and again daily. The good news is, you can change your thought patterns. The bad news is, it takes diligence and work.

What could be more enjoyable, however, than the work involved in reorganizing your thought patterns to send desirable thoughts to your subconscious? These desirable thoughts then become your desirable life, and isn't that the point? At some point in your life, you have to put the books down, go to a seminar or workshop, and begin to put everything you have learned into action on a daily basis. You can start with recognizing the power of emotional expectation.

The subconscious is the center for universal consciousness within you. As your desire heightens emotionally, there will come a point when the emotional intensity is what acts to move matter and manifest that which you desire. Once you get your thoughts on track, backing them up with strong emotional intensity is what really lights the fire of creation.

Rearrange your thoughts so they are positive, this is essential. The emotional aspect is also essential, however. It is not enough to just be aware of your thoughts and re-phrase them in a positive way if you are really adamant about achieving your dreams and the life you desire. You must back up the positive thoughts with strong emotion of expectation. The expectation will release the dopamine, which will contribute to your feeling good throughout the process. The underlying emotion behind the thought propels the thought into creation.

How do you ensure that the underlying emotion will be a positive one? This is the tricky part. Think back to a time in your life when you felt confident, or happy. Now think back to a time in your life when you felt sad. What happens with many people is they find they are unable to get over things like divorce, or loss, or other challenges, because they continue to revisit the sadness or negative emotion that was present during the event. I want to show you how you can call up your past emotions and use them for good; to propel your life forward in a positive way. The insidious cognitive cancer that affects all of us happens when we set up the law of expectation and emotionalize the thought out of our past experiences, and use negative emotions.

Emotions can be borrowed from our past experiences and applied to our current experiences. Imagine you are a tennis player. You expected to win your last match, you did win your last match, and the win provided you with a positive emotion and confidence. Now, to access that emotion and use it to your advantage, take a moment to quiet your mind. Recall the alpha state techniques I explained in chapter 8, and do this when you are in a similar state. Allow yourself to access a positive emotion from your past. For example, access the time you wanted to date that girl and you did, or the time you won your baseball game, or the time you wanted to pass your exam and you did. With this exercise, we are going to borrow the emotion from the past, and future pace it into the present. In your mind's eye, create a horizontal line. And picture that line so that right in front of you is the present moment. And picture a small circle on the line. Move the circle to the left, similar to a volume control on a stereo, and access an emotion attached to a word - words like confidence, love, joy - something positive and meaningful to you. Now, picture your mind going back perhaps one month, perhaps one year, perhaps two years, or more. Take yourself back. And when you get to an event where you were confident, in love, joyful, (or whatever word you chose), bask in that moment. Become emotionally aware of how you felt. Memory is infallible, and the subconscious never forgets anything; so allow it to do its work, and access that emotion.

Now that you feel that emotion - let's say it's confidence - take that confidence, and in your mind's, eye put it in the little circle on your line. Supercharge the circle with your energetics of confidence and the feelings of confidence. Begin to slide the circle now, filled with your confidence, to the right - until it lands in front of you again - in the present moment. Take that little circle filled and infused with confidence, and pull it into your heading, using a technique known as an absorption protocol. Essentially, what you will have done is installed confidence in the present by borrowing confidence from the past. This is a very powerful and effective way to emotionalize your thoughts and attract what you want to you in your life.

That's not all, however! Now, let's do some future pacing. Imagine a time in the future where you want to succeed. Maybe you have a golf game coming up that you hope to win. You can imagine the event in the future, and take that same circle infused with your confidence and move it along the line to the right of your present moment, and energetically charge the event. You are now anchoring in your subconscious the confidence from the past and inserting it into your present.

Emotion is energy; energy has no lifespan, it is only transformed. By pushing this emotion into your future, when you go to your golf game you will now have an elevated sense of confidence. Essentially we are borrowing our emotions from the past to fuel our expectation. We can craft the future by maximizing the present through this technique.

Let's do it again. Put that little circle back on the line, close your eyes, see that circle at the present moment. Move that circle to the left until you access a past point in time where you experienced the emotion of love. Bask in the emotion, how good it felt, how inviting. Infuse that little circle with the remembered emotion, and travel it back along the line to present time. Move the circle perhaps a little into the future, and think about the person you have a crush on, or even a place or thing you want to love and look forward to loving. Borrow the emotion, move it into the future and anchor that emotion to a future event.

Simply put, the thoughts are the match. The intention is striking the match, and the emotion is the gasoline that turns the spark of thought into an inferno of results. This is the most basic formula when understanding the power of emotional expectation in creating the life you dream of and attracting all that you seek.

There is a caveat, of course. You must control your emotions. Once you see how emotion hangs on to people, places, locations, events, you must learn to spot when you have anchored negative emotions to an experience. Anchoring negative emotions to an experience is like polluting a beautiful, pristine lake.

What do I mean by anchoring negative emotions to experiences? Do you get into your car and feel angry, regardless of the day or what's happening? This is a common example. What is happening here is that you had an experience in your car, stuck in traffic, or in an accident or something that made you angry, and you now feel that anger every time you get in the car. Do you hate your job? Whatever may have happened to you at work may have left the emotion of hate towards the workplace and anchored it to your job, so that you always feel that emotion when you think of work. To change this, simply use the technique I outlined above again, and move the little circle all the way to the left until you access something about that job that brought you happiness or joy. Move that happiness back over on the line to your present. Using thought dilution, you can make the emotion and thought less omnipotent. Nothing is omnipotent! With this process, you can clean your slate so you can quantum leap your thought processes and get to the creation of your reality faster.

To contact Jim:

info@lutesinternational.com

www.lutesinternational.com

www.jimluteslive.com

The Change 2

Tina Sanchoo

If you're in a position where you have to make big decisions; considering making a big life change; are going through a transition in a relationship, career or a move; or you are just looking to make your current life "sizzle" - then Tina Sanchoo can definitely help you.

She is an Internationally Certified Lifestyle and Success Coach, who delights in empowering her clients to live extraordinary lives and fulfill their dreams with intention and joy. Passionate about personal development and success, Tina has a natural way of bringing out people's greatness with enthusiasm, authenticity, humor and incredible heart.

Throughout the coaching process, Tina works with clients to examine their present situation, explore their current and future options, and to get a clear understanding about what they want and how they can get it. She absolutely loves the experience of being with another person in a space that is created by trust, vision and commitment.

Tina's New York City practice has expanded to include national and international clients via phone and Skype. She offers a complimentary first session to connect and establish compatibility - and set future coaching goals with a clear and concise action plan for its attainment.

The Power of Surrender

By Tina Sanchoo

"To hold, you must first open your hand. Let go."
- Lao Tzu

Originally, my intention was to write this chapter on embracing change, and in the spirit of doing so - I had a change of heart. I decided to let it all go and give into a very familiar feeling - a feeling of calmness, stillness and love. It's something I've been working on very diligently for the past two and a half years… Surrender.

Deepak Chopra, one of my personal mentors, once said, "Surrender is faith, that the power of love can accomplish anything even when you cannot foresee the outcome." Those words always touch my heart and soothe me – releasing me from my concerns and bringing a feeling of peace. To me, surrender is the willingness to say yes to every moment. To be present. To trust the moment. The Now. And to not argue with reality, because when I deny reality, I suffer - sometimes very deeply!

Surrender will bring to you many gifts including the big "F" word: Freedom! It brings ever-increasing joy, contentment, acceptance, peace and lightness! To be in a state of surrender means that you will be free of negative feelings - allowing creativity and spontaneity to manifest without the resistance or interference from internal conflicts.

The more you surrender, you become less encumbered by stress. And we all know what stress causes!

So now you're probably thinking, "This sounds great and all but how do I begin the journey of Surrender?" In this chapter, I want to share some deeply personal pointers that helped me to literally "survive" surrender. What I can tell you, with certainty, is that you can do it too – because you've been doing it your whole life – especially, when you are given no other choice!

Step One: Expect the Unexpected

My greatest lesson with surrender began on June 6, 2013. That was the day I received the phone call. The one I feared the most! My phone rang at about 5:20pm and my sister was on the other end of the line. All she said was, "Get to the hospital now." She was crying hysterically! I was five minutes away. My thirteen-year-old niece Hema and I began to run – the fastest we could, and when we got there - it was too late! My mother just died.

I was numb. I cried and I cried, until there was no water left in my body to produce tears. My heart hurt like it never did before. I think the worst moment I had during that time was about five hours after the funeral. I had taken a nap and when I woke up – reality started setting in! I felt the loss severely! I felt the constriction in my throat and the pain in my heart. And the tears didn't stop flowing. I was struggling to understand what happened and felt the intense pain of her not being here anymore. I can tell you sincerely, THAT moment was the most painful moment of my life!

As the days went by, I was able to function better but I didn't feel like I was getting better. I thought I was moving forward on certain days, but then I fell right back down, struggling to get up. I felt abandoned, betrayed, and simply left. I intellectually knew that my mother didn't leave by choice - but my heart didn't understand. It was a time in my life that I didn't know who I was anymore. I felt very unsupported. The friends that were close to me for the longest time were not around. I am the youngest of seven siblings and during that time, everyone in my family stuck to themselves. My little nieces and nephews were the greatest support to me especially, Hema. But, still I felt alone – and this is the first lesson of surrender. Sometimes you just have to accept that there are things in life you cannot control – as painful as that might be!

Step Two: Surrender to help from where it comes – not where you expect it to come from.

About six months later, my friend Ashish was visiting New York City, where I live, from Atlanta. We made plans to meet. He had been calling me for hours but I wasn't answering the phone. I was intensely feeling the pain of separation from my mom, especially with the holidays approaching. I didn't want to break down on the phone with him as I was always known as the one who held it all together. I finally answered because I started to feel guilty. I opened up to him and starting crying. Trying to justify my reasons for crying, I suddenly felt a very deep knowing inside of me - "Maybe it's because I've known her for thirty four years and how can I possibly expect to feel better in only six months. She's been with me my entire life and maybe it will take another 34 years for me to feel better!" As I spoke these words to Ashish, I immediately felt something shift inside of me. My tears started to subside. I understood that my mother was a part of me. She was in my blood. My DNA. Every cell of my body. Had I not spoken to him – had I not let go and allowed myself to accept help from someone who was trying to be there for me – I may never have come to that realization!

That evening, I sat quietly in my room and asked the Universe for help. The words "I Surrender" came out of me and I just kept on saying it over and over. I asked for guidance and help in healing my extremely broken heart. I woke up every morning with the prayer for someone / something / anything to help me, heal me and guide me. My intention and my theme since then has been surrender - not just for my mother, but for everything else in my life.

Step Three: Surrender to Physical, Mental and Spiritual Practices that Support You

As time went by, it became a bit easier as I was very committed to my surrender. I started putting full effort into going out and socializing, although I didn't want to. It was hard, really hard, but I had a greater purpose and so I kept on asking for spiritual guidance – and that is where "co-incidence" began to emerge! I was led to a study group for the book, A Course in Miracles. Although I felt a ginormous amount of resistance inside of me to do something new, I dove in deep! I attended every week because it was simple, profound and extremely healing. I also made my workouts a priority at the gym because I noticed how down and out I felt when I didn't go. There were times when I went to the gym in tears and left in tears! I'm sure some of the other members thought I was sweating on the stair climber, but many of those times, I was actually crying. It was pure emotional release!

Step Four: Sometimes to Surrender – You Have to Be a Fighter

There was a boxing class I had been eyeing at the gym for many years, but I'd felt scared to even step foot in the room! I watched it from the outside and always said, "One day." Well, that one day came at 6:30 am one Tuesday morning as I stepped into the jungle! It was hard, I was scared, but I still went. The instructor for the class was Jenaro Diaz - he was a warrior! At some point during the class, I was at the wrong end of the rotation line to box with him. Usually, the newbies go first after the warm up because, well, they usually suck - as I did! He didn't know I was new. I didn't know newbies went first. And after about an hour of some intense army style training, it was my turn with the warrior. Let's just say that I learned the importance of breathing about two minutes later! He had his mitts, I had my gloves and he was teaching me - pushing me to go beyond my limits. All I remember is him saying, "faster, faster, faster," and the next thing I remembered was that I was sitting on the floor leaning up against the wall. I didn't know what happened and for a quick second I didn't know where I was either. As my vision and hearing returned completely, I saw everyone around me asking if I was ok. Later that day, I found out that Jenaro had been teaching that class for 20 years and a lot of the people in the class were veteran boxers!

I was embarrassed. But, it didn't last for very long because for some strange reason, I wanted to go back! Everyone was surprised because usually the newbies don't return - especially having had the experience that I had! I was scared every single time for many months. I had to keep overcoming the "logical excuses" as to why I shouldn't go. But whenever I got there, he would look at me and say, "Are you ready killer?" and I always said, "Yes!" Time after time, I would surprise myself! I didn't know where the power, endurance and stamina came from. The days I wasn't feeling my best were the days I amazed myself even more. Jenaro always told me, "All you have to do is show up, no matter what, and everything else will work out." I've heard that and I "knew-knew" it - but boxing became my proof and my therapy!

From that day onwards, I acknowledged all of my fears and excuses. I surrendered them over and over because for some strange reason, although I was scared, I was also compelled to go back to that man's class! Shortly after, I started training privately with him when I realized how incredibly disciplined, committed and strong I had become in every area of my life from being in his presence!

Step Five: Sometimes Surrender Means Just "Shutting Up"

One of the biggest tips I can give you on surrendering is the importance of meditation. It can be as simple as sitting silently with your eyes closed and taking long, slow, deep breaths. And witnessing yourself. Your thoughts. Your behavior. The more chaotic things are on the outside, the more still you need to get on the inside. Meditation takes me out of the past and the future – where most of us spend our time – and brings me to the present moment where I can be consciously aware of what's really happening. I have been a mediator for over 10 years and my daily practice was most helpful during this time. When my mom died, a lot of the hurt came from feelings of abandonment. I felt feelings of betrayal and some things that I can't put into words. Eventually, when I got a grasp on myself, I began questioning my thoughts and feelings by asking "Is it true?" Is it true that my mom abandoned me? Is it really true? I continuously asked that question over and over until the energy attached to those troubling thoughts and feelings began to diffuse. This very simple question has transformed my perspective and my life – sometimes instantaneously!

I can tell you endless stories about surrender and its role in my life since childhood. It's when I intentionally and actively chose it everyday that I really took charge of my life, and purposefully hand-picked everything in it. I was committed, disciplined and courageous in doing everything I could to move towards my healing.

Step Six: Relationships are to Surrender - What Fish Hooks are to Fish!

Almost as challenging of an experience was the death of my romantic relationship – it was excruciating! I say this because it felt like there was a fish hook tugging at my heart constantly. When we met, it seemed clear that somehow we were destined to meet exactly where we did, exactly how we did. It had been years in the making when I connected all the dots of how everything had to line up for that grand meeting.

Our relationship was very intense and very spiritual. We connected on levels that I had never before experienced and we had the greatest time together! It felt "royal" and it was sexy! We inspired each other to be the best of ourselves and were committed to being great in the world - and with each other. But, what I have learned is that when you are in a romantic relationship with someone – eventually, all of your dirty laundry will come to light and the skeletons will creep out of the closet! Everything you need to work on will be brought to the surface. Slowly, our relationship started having complications, schedules got hectic and communication was misunderstood. There was a lot of talk that wasn't followed through with action on his part, which troubled me, because I try very hard to be a woman of my word.

He said he would never let me fall. That he would always show up for me. Always be there. Always keep his word and always do his best. None of those things were happening and eventually, we had what would be our last conversation - on the phone. I decided that I would no longer bear the pain of the relationship. And when I had that moment of knowing I had to stop, completely stop – surrender came in! And I gave it all away!

At that time, I felt like I did something wrong. That something was not right with me. And that's why it didn't work. Feelings of unworthiness and "I'm not good enough" surfaced. I felt betrayed and lost. Although, I just wanted to lay in bed and wallow in misery all day, I forced myself to get up and do things to keep me moving forward in a positive way. I made a decision, for my healing and well being, that I would not contact him. I surrounded myself with motivation. I cut out photos of inspiration and taped them everywhere in my home. This Rumi quote, "Live life as though it is rigged in your favor" gave me faith when I didn't have any. And this one was fierce! "Let go or be dragged." Well, that said it all!

I also read a book by David Hawkins, with a chapter on "The Anatomy of Emotions." A machine was utilized to measure the electronic vibrations of people experiencing various emotions. I was really excited that there were actual "scientific measurements" which could help me understand what was happening with me. From looking at the scale of vibrations, Peace was at the top of the list with a vibration of 600 hertz. Joy was 540 hertz. Love was 500 hertz. At the very bottom of the scale were Guilt, with a vibration of 30 hertz and Shame at 20 hertz.

At that moment, I felt like I had an epiphany! The man I was with was amazing in many ways. Mr. Amazing was always full of life! He served the world in an incredible way with his work and he always had a gorgeous smile on his face. BUT, Mr. Amazing was also carrying the lowest energetic vibrations on the scale! Hawkins says, shame and guilt are characterized by "playing dead," humiliation, desire to punish and be punished - leading to self-sabotage, cruelty, self-hatred and rejection among other things. Something clicked inside of me at that moment and my "inner knowing" made its appearance. A very soft, beautiful voice inside of me said, "You know, it wasn't you. You didn't do anything wrong. It would've never worked no matter what because he never worked on all of his guilt. He didn't lie to you or betray you. He only betrayed himself." I realized as long as he was carrying those emotions along in his energy field, we would repel each other! At that moment, I felt something left my body. This black hole inside of me started filling up with joy. I instantly felt lighter! I learned that in order for relationships to work, you have to be on the same vibration!

Step Seven: When the Student is Ready to Surrender – the Teacher Will Appear

During that time I met many great teachers, including Gerry Gavin, who has become a great mentor and friend. He always reminded me that "Courage is surrender to the unknown." Gerry channels an angel named Margaret and performed a Soul Retrieval for me. This is a Shamanic practice that brings back pieces of your life force that may get lost when you go through traumatic changes that make you feel powerless. It helped tremendously!

At the same time, I was also led to the Kabbalah Centre in New York City and my studies there have been exceptionally transformative! I also began learning Red and White Tantra – which had been on my "to-learn" list for many years. I deeply immersed myself into Kundalini Yoga, another item on my "to-learn" list. Kundalini and Tantra both have completely transformed my mind, body and soul tenfold! I know some of this may sound a little "out-there" – however, I found that all of this work is grounded in some very clear Science and Physics.

Step Eight: Remain in Thankfulness

Whenever I felt challenged by occurrences, I focused on how much I learned from my mother and my romantic relationship – and how much I grew from it all! Sadness began to leave quickly because I remained in thankfulness always! I had my gratitude journal out every day and wrote all of the things I was thankful for every morning and night. It always took me out of lack and into a state of affluence instantly, because when I went through my day looking for things to be grateful for - something always appeared! And that brought more goodness into my life because I focused on everything I already had instead of what I didn't have. Gratitude has been the simplest, fastest, most compelling way to create positive change in my life!

This journey has transformed and empowered me in miraculous ways and I am so thankful for it! My deepest struggles produced my greatest strengths! I still surrender my life to The Divine, for it to be used for the greatest service to humanity. I practice self-compassion and self-appreciation diligently. As a result, my self-love skyrocketed and it was as if I began a love affair with myself! True surrender brought me to a place in my life where I am so proud of who I've become, and my hope is that everyone can experience this feeling of exhilaration!

Writing this was not easy for me. I debated over and over whether I should scrap it and write about something else. In the end, I decided to surrender and be deeply real with you. I hope that sharing my personal story of surrender has been helpful for you. Loss is not easy and relationships are not easy – if that is the story that you believe. I learned to change that story for myself and it has been magical! Working with my clients, I guide them to be comfortable with honestly exploring their stories to create brand new, empowering ones for themselves. Stories where they are not powerless, like a leaf being tossed about in the wind - but rather a story where they are like a strong tree, firmly rooted in a powerful foundation - branching out into successful and joyous lives!

To contact Tina Sanchoo:

>Website: www.tinasanchoo.com
>Email: hello@tinasanchoo.com
>Facebook: www.facebook.com/tsanchoo

The Change 2

Andrea Isaacs

Andrea Isaacs established her expertise in the field of emotional intelligence when she created EnneaMotion and Somatic Focusing in 1994. Since then, she has guided thousands of growth-oriented individuals to personal mastery and inspired leadership. As a direct result of her teaching and coaching, her clients have been attracting, creating and manifesting productive, impassioned lives - with effectiveness, efficiency and joy - both professionally and personally. Using her approach to increasing emotional intelligence, she transformed her own painful shyness into the confidence to speak to and coach thousands of people around the world. She has been on the Enneagram Institute faculty since 1994, was on the board of directors for the International Enneagram Association for six years, and was co-founding editor/publisher of the *Enneagram Monthly*. She is the author of the forthcoming eBook: *Body Wisdom, the Enneagram and Emotional Intelligence: Embodying Your Best Self*. In her collaboration with neuro-science researcher, Dario Nardi, they have found her work brings on wholeness and inner peace in the brain

..

Body Wisdom:
for Creating Lasting Change

By Andrea Isaacs

Have you reacted emotionally in a relationship or job and wish you hadn't? I have taught and coached thousands of people around the world, and have learned that emotional reactivity is the most pervasive challenge to many people's professional and personal lives. It can be tough when you experience anger, shyness, anxiety, etc., despite "knowing better," and it feels even worse when you compound the problem with self-criticism. How can you change your deep habits and triggers in a lasting way?

When leading a workshop exercise, a woman I'll call Maia started to cry. I approached her gently, and she agreed to work with me to learn and grow by working with her spontaneous reaction. The exercise had evoked feelings of sadness and rage, and she said she felt like hiding under a chair. So we started there.

It was clear Maia wanted to stay hidden; she felt safe. I asked her if there was something, anything "out there" that she wanted in her life. She said "Yes." I asked her to crawl out from under the chair and go for it. Motivated, she moved with determination. As she started to crawl out, I put my hands on her shoulders to make forward movement difficult. It was as if I were creating for Maia the cage she had created for herself and had been living inside of her whole life.

I coached her to press forward against this resistance with her "hidden smallness," as if she had to carry it with her throughout her day and throughout her life. The strain and effort felt very familiar to her. Suddenly, something shifted energetically inside her and I was compelled to let go. And there she was — almost unrecognizable. She stood tall with her feet spread wide, her spine elongated, shoulders broad and her two fists stacked on top of each other in front of her belly. I asked her to find a phrase to help anchor that energy in her mind and body. She said, "I have a sturdy core and I AM HERE." In that moment, there was no doubt about this woman's presence and her ability to hold her ground.

Neither one of us would ever have thought of a phrase like that! It came to her because she was listening to the wisdom of her body.

Maia didn't know it, but she had discovered for herself a mantra and a mudra that would change her life. Together, they served as a powerful antidote for her to use the next time she felt small, insignificant or angry. Years later when I saw her, she reported that she was continuing to use her mantra and mudra and that they had indeed changed her life.

What did Maia uncover? Why does it work? How can anyone do this? Let's look more closely, starting with the common barriers to changing our emotional habits.

Why is Change So Difficult?

Regardless of our best intentions, there are three major barriers to change that we need to understand and address to disarm our emotional triggers. I discovered techniques that do this on my own journey in transforming the painful shyness of my youth into confidence, and I have fine-tuned them into easy-to-use steps by teaching them for over 20 years.

Barrier #1: We know the **What** but Not the **How**

People often know (or others tell them) *what* they should do differently, and they can describe it plainly. But the *what* does not necessarily include the *how*. As a recovering shy person, when my buttons were pushed, my habit was to withdraw, shut down and not speak, even when surrounded by the people I most wanted to connect with. My shyness was so great that I would wish the earth would open up beneath me so I could fall in, as if being in the bowels of the earth would be more comfortable than being seen. I would often withdraw or simply be dead quiet. I didn't like the isolation of not connecting, so I would tell myself to stop it, to speak up, and to engage more with others. I knew *what* I wanted to do, but didn't know *how*. My old shy pattern would kick in, strengthened by years of practice, and I found myself saying, "Oh no! I did it again! I HATE it when I do that."

I had a client I'll call Hans who had an anger problem and often yelled at his young children. They would cry and became afraid of him. He deeply regretted this pattern. He saw he was pushing them away, which was the last thing he wanted to do. He loved them and wanted a better relationship with them. He just didn't know *how*.

Somehow we need to discover *how* to achieve the "way of being" that we desire.

Barrier #2: We Don't Have the Neural Pathways

Neural pathways are like highways that transport information from your brain to your body and from your body back to your brain. The thoughts, feelings and actions you engage in most often travel along strong and well-developed pathways and represent what you are good at. As you develop skills and habits, you have well-established pathways for knowing how to get dressed, solve a difficult problem, act with confidence, etc. The inverse is also true. If you don't think, feel or behave in those ways, you won't have a strong neural pathway for them. It will seem unfamiliar, difficult or inaccessible. We may also have habitually wired our brain to experience qualities we don't necessarily want, like shyness, anxiety, impatience, etc. Hans did not want to scold and scare his children, but he had a strong and well-practiced neural pathway for anger and had not developed a more useful pathway of patient listening and loving discipline.

The good news is that your patterns and habits are not etched in stone in the brain. Your brain has "neuroplasticity" - the ability to be molded in new ways through conscious practice and the ability to create new neural pathways.

We need a way to develop *new neural pathways* that produce the habits we most desire.

<u>Barrier #3</u>: We Don't Know How to Develop Our Emotional Intelligence

Emotional Intelligence (EQ) is the ability to perceive, understand, and manage the world of emotions and feelings. EQ is the key to managing your own emotional life and your relationships with others with good judgment and empathy.

If you increase your emotional range and flexibility, you will become less emotionally reactive and able to respond effectively, resourcefully, and with resilience *in any circumstances, no matter what life throws at you* - even in the face of what had been a trigger.

In summary, to increase our EQ, we need to:

- Learn the *how* behind *what* we want to do differently;
- Develop neural pathways to build new habits;
- Increase our emotional resilience to expand our range and flexibility of responses.

It all has to do with listening to our body's wisdom.

And We Can - Learn How to Listen to the Body's Wisdom!

I will give you an overview of what I've developed during the past 20 years of learning, experimenting and teaching. I have had the great privilege of being inspired by many talented mentors and teachers, and hope to contribute the best of what I've learned and created to you.

My Body Wisdom approach includes two methods - EnneaMotion and Somatic Focusing.

EnneaMotion

EnneaMotion has its intellectual roots in the Enneagram. The Enneagram is a personality system that describes nine different patterns of thinking, feeling and engaging with the world. Each type, or style, has its own set of predictable gifts and challenges. The Enneagram is useful for understanding the wide variety of our experiences. It is a brilliant, time-tested framework for increasing understanding of, and compassion for ourselves and others. It can shed bright light and insight into our deepest habits.

After studying the Enneagram for many years, I found that knowing about the nine types was useful, but it didn't help me build new habits of emotional resilience. Drawing on many years of experience as a choreographer, I combined the body's ability to move in a way that makes us feel different emotions, with the range of emotions inherent in the Enneagram system.

I initially created EnneaMotion as a way to learn the lessons of the nine Enneagram types in a bone-deep way. I quickly realized it was much more than that. Because it engages the body, EnneaMotion engages the brain to develop new neural pathways for the expression of the healthy attributes of *all* the personality types. This was literally expanding our emotional repertoire. This is what resilience needs - emotional range to support not always responding the way we always responded.

In EnneaMotion, you explore each of the nine Enneagram types to understand the advantages and resources of each. Through a series of exercises, you explore the best of each type as well as the pitfalls or "shadow side" of each. We all have the potential to utilize the advantages and suffer the disadvantages of each personality type, so it is worthwhile to get to know the whole variety of personalities distinguished by the Enneagram.

The Power of Mantra and Mudra

Mantra and *mudra* are both Sanskrit terms. Traditionally a *mantra* is a word or phrase that induces a state of resourceful awareness. "Om" is perhaps the most well-known mantra for meditation, but I believe that *any* word or phrase that enhances your awareness, focus, and a resourceful intention can serve as a useful personal mantra.

Traditionally, a *mudra* is a prayer or meditation position used to enhance your inner state. I believe that you can custom-design a body position that expresses and amplifies your desired inner state.

As I guide you through the EnneaMotion exercises, you will experience a wide variety of body sensations. Certain movements (mudras) and phrases (mantras) will seem natural and powerful to you. Through the care and support of other participants, along with my facilitation, you will develop for each type a specific, personal mudra and mantra (M&M) that will help you gain immediate access to the healthy attributes you desire the most for your personal development. By the end of the EnneaMotion program, you will have developed and practiced a custom-designed set of nine M&Ms. Through regular practice, your M&Ms will train and strengthen new neural pathways, expand your comfort zone, increase your emotional resilience, and thus support your deep and lasting change.

Change happens by creating and using the neural pathways that represent and support the change you want to make.

From Shy to Confident: An EnneaMotion Exercise

I'll never forget the first time I taught EnneaMotion. We were doing the exercise for type Eight, sometimes called the Boss, the Leader, or the Challenger. At their best, Eights are grounded, warm, decisive, direct, magnanimous, bold and naturally confident. At their worst, they're controlling bullies, and their short anger fuse can turn to rage.

We started to do the exercise exploring the challenges, or the lower qualities of type Eight. The room exploded in anger and rage. A man, much larger than me, approached and screamed at me, while striking and flinging his arms. I got scared. I looked for the door and wanted to run. I only stopped myself when I said, "You can't leave; you're the facilitator!" So I stayed, in terror. And then realized, "Oh, this is just an exercise! I can do that back to him!" Since I had created the exercise, you would think I'd have known that! But my fear was so real I had forgotten. So I did, or rather, I tried to muster up the energy to express some of that anger and rage back at him, but my attempt was pretty feeble. I felt a profound sense of loss because my neural pathway to express anger had been so neglected.

By exploring the shadow side of type Eight, I learned to strengthen my neural pathway for expressing anger. That doesn't mean I now have license to go out and express rage whenever I'm angry - NO! It does mean that I'm no longer afraid of the energy of anger. I learned that anger is just energy. It happens to be a *lot* of energy. The exercise taught me that nothing terrible would happen to me or by me if I allowed myself to experience that much energy. After becoming less fearful, it became possible for me to stand in the energy of anger, my own or someone else's, without having to yell, scream or run away. I could hold my ground and speak with confidence.

As you explore the Enneagram types that you're less familiar with, you may experience some surprising gifts. This exercise gave me a wonderful gift - an antidote to my shyness. My personal mudra for type Eight was standing with feet firmly planted, shoulders pressed down into my back, belly center engaged, with my hands pressed down towards the earth. My personal mantra became: *I hold my ground and speak my voice.* This was huge in embodying my confidence, and has changed my life.

Like Maia, this is another example of how a mantra and mudra created during an EnneaMotion exercise created greater resilience, increased emotional intelligence and supported lasting change.

Somatic Focusing

Somatic Focusing is the second Body Wisdom system I created. It's a form of alchemy, but instead of transforming lead into gold, we transform emotions we don't like into emotions we do like. It uses the same core strategies as EnneaMotion:

- translate emotional energy into physical energy;
- listen to the body's wisdom; and

- anchor the preferred feeling with an M&M.

From Anger to Connection: An Example

Remember Hans, mentioned earlier, who was angry with himself for yelling at his young children. I asked what his body felt like when he was angry. He said his energy was hard and fast; his jaw was tight, every muscle in his face was contracted, his hands were clenched in fists, his energy felt very fast, he felt like striking out, and there was a lot of energy in his whole body.

In real life, Hans had often yelled at his children. They would cry and become afraid of him. He was sad and confused about his reactivity, and felt terrible about alienating them. The core issue was never resolved, and they were all left with underlying resentment.

Hans wanted to change; he wanted a different result. As you know, if you'd like to change *how* you handle challenging situations, *you have to do something different.*

When change is difficult, it's important to by-pass the thinking mind and to listen to the body's wisdom. *And so I asked Hans what his body would rather feel.* As he focused on listening to his body's wisdom, there was a softening of his energy; he let that softer energy spread throughout his body. He started to feel something stirring in his heart center. Energy follows attention, so I invited him to focus his mind's attention there.

To understand the body's language, you must notice whatever sensation starts to arise in answer to this question, and to exaggerate whatever that is, allowing your body to respond to that impulse.

Eventually, his body settled in a position that captured the feeling he wanted. His arms were thrown back so far that his sternum (or heart center) was splayed wide open. It looked like his heart had literally cracked open. He was lunging forward. His head was thrown back, and then he brought both palms to his heart center, as if reminding himself to soften his energy. In doing that, he remembered his love for his children.

By *letting his body inform his mind,* he anchored this sensation by feeling this new energy in his body, and completing an "I" statement, like: "I . . . " or "I am . . . " or "I have . . . "

The mantra Hans came up with was, "I speak gently from my heart."

With his M&M, he can still ask his children to pick up after themselves. He doesn't have to yell or scream, or repress his thoughts, but rather he can speak from a place of tenderness that leads to a deeper connection with his children.

As the M&M is practiced and repeated, the new neural pathway becomes stronger and new emotions become more available. The mantra can eventually be spoken quietly in the mind. Once the neural pathway is established, the mere thought of your mantra is enough to activate the pathway; this *will* change how you think, feel and engage with life.

The BODY WISDOM methods of EnneaMotion and Somatic Focusing are easy-to-use techniques that create new neural pathways that support lasting change.

Now It's Your Turn

You really can change your habits to become less reactive and more emotionally responsive. By exploring a wide range of emotional responses, for instance through the diverse types of the Enneagram, you can create your *"how"* for desired change: creating new neural pathways for greater emotional range, flexibility and resilience - the components of increasing your emotional intelligence. It's not hard or strenuous, but it takes a thorough exploration of yourself and the willingness to develop and practice your new *mantras* (phrases) and *mudras* (body positions).

Your body has the wisdom you need to create the change you want.

Go to www.EnneaMotion.com for more information, Andrea's schedule, and a free audio of Andrea being interviewed by Katie Hendricks for the Shift Network's "Body Intelligence Summit." She can be reached at Andrea@EnneaMotion.com

Antonetta Fernandes

Antonetta Fernandes is a Best Selling Author, Life Coach/mentor, Public Speaker, Angelic Reiki Healer and self professed Queen of Manifestation. Her first co-authored book *The Giant Within* made the best sellers list in two categories. Antonetta's currently co-authored book *The Journey Behind*, has had great reviews and press releases, and is heading for the same success.

Born in Kenya, the eldest of 9 siblings, she experienced her first claim to fame as an artist at 16. During the course of her career, Antonetta has worked with national & international companies. Her involvement with "Convergence 97" at London Television Studios, gave her a head start in embracing the internet, social media and mobile technology with industry leaders and gurus.

Antonetta's dynamic skills and passion has driven her philanthropic projects. As editor of West London Goans, she took on a taboo campaign against the Child Sex Trade in Goa in 1996. The campaign gathered momentum in the United Kingdom and around the world. In her spare time, she vigorously works with charitable organizations raising funds for the street children in Brazil, water wells in West Africa, Aids orphanage in Uganda, and Leprosy home in Mauritius. In 2000, she completed the Dublin Marathon, raising £3000 for Whizz Kids, a charity that provides customized wheelchairs. She graduated from the Academy of Wealth & Achievement as a Master Results Coach, NLP Master Practitioner, NLP Trainer, Hypnotherapist and Performance Consultant.

A Voice Awakened

By Antonetta Fernandes

"Your speech was an ideal combination of motivation and humor." "Thank you so much for your wonderful keynote presentation!" "Dynamic, humorous and inspiring." "Your contribution is the icing on the cake…" and so on and so forth. These are the compliments/testimonials I had dreamt of hearing if only I could find this voice that had stayed dormant for so long. Why is it so easy for a small minority to have the gift of the gab while the majority of us struggle to get an idea out at team meetings or when presenting and giving speeches? How many of us say, "I would rather die than speak in public?"

Reflecting back on my childhood in Kenya, I remember my mother always speaking up for a cause or a need, and to this day, will still voice an opinion. My grandma, of what little I remember of her, was totally outspoken and took no prisoners. So, I cannot use the excuse that culturally in Indian families, women do not have a voice. At times, I used to feel to sorry for my father as he tried to get across a point in between my mother and grandma; he did not have a hope in hell of standing firm on a decision.

In school, my yearly reports were very good mostly, and how I avoided reading out loud in class was an art I mastered with so many excuses. My three favorite subjects were English Literature, World History and

Art. English Literature gave me the love of listening to well-written plays - for example, Shakespeare's Merchant of Venice, Macbeth, and The Tempest - and coupled with the passion for acting in the poems of Elizabeth Barrett-Browning, "How do I love thee, let me count the ways" being my top poem to this day. I would spend hours daydreaming, moving in and out of the different roles, acting out the characters, reciting the words to perfection with gusto and passion. In this wonderful cocoon, I saw myself on stage reciting this poem to millions around the world as Elizabeth Barrett-Browning in her all regalia and Victorian costumes of the nineteenth century.

In 1974, I left Kenya at the age of 22 and started my married life in the outskirts of London. I was happy to start my first employment in a factory assembling lights bulbs where my brother and husband worked, rather than registering with an employment agency for an office administration position, of which I was petrified. Twice I made an attempt to register, and both times I walked out. A kind soul saw the fear I had of speaking up, held my hand and helped me through the process of finding a position in an office.

My career flourished. My working life was great. I was climbing the corporate ladder swiftly, and I always managed to blind side the fear of speaking at meetings voicing an opinion to the detriment of even correcting my name, which has been spelt wrong for so long. However, a manager helped me out here when he saw a certificate I had received for my achievement. He thought they had spelt my name wrong. So a memorandum went around to all departments to inform them that my name was Antonetta and not Antoinette. It was difficult for my work colleagues to acknowledge my correct name and equally difficult for me too to hear the correct pronunciation after 15 years of service in this organization. My home life with my son and husband was totally different; at home I controlled and managed the household. I wrote all my husband's speeches, as he was the President of our local community club. He got accolades for his speeches. In 2000, my marriage fell apart and there was this desperate need to speak up. My journey to finding a solution to facing up to my fears had finally started.

According to Statistic Brain, the fear of public speaking is known as Glossophobia. The word originates from the Greek word *glōssa,* meaning tongue, and *phobos,* meaning fear or dread. Public Speaking is the number one phobia in the world - even greater than death; Statistic Brain further confirms 74% of people in USA suffer from speech anxiety i.e. 75% of women and 73% of men. While I was searching for this magic pill, I was given a gift, just like manna from heaven. At a 3-day personal development event, I manifested and won £7000 ($11,110) worth of training.

I qualified as a Master Neuro Linguistic Practitioner, Hypnotherapist and a Life Coach. It is during the extensive practical training, I was able to take on board that we are not born with this fear and it most certainly is not part of my physiological or psychological make up. Understanding the concept of NLP, I needed no persuasion in hiring an NLP Master Result coach. NLP (Neuro Linguistic Programming) was developed in the late 1960's and early 1970's by computer scientist Richard Bandler, and linguist John Grinder. NLP has proven to be a reliable, fast way for people like me to gain control of the mind and therefore get the desired results. The biggest shift I got was understanding Cause and Effect, followed by strategic visioning and working with sub-modalities elicitation.

My first presentation was nerve-racking. The start was a bit petrifying, but I kept it together and was very proud of the delivery. It was my second day in this job, so my colleague had no idea of my phobia of speaking in a group, let alone doing a presentation. My confidence grew with each meeting and workshop I took part in, and I was so grateful to be able to contribute with my ideas. Now it is one thing to do a presentation at work with people you know, but talking in public to an audience is a different kettle of fish.

I recall going to Hyde Park, the original Speakers' Corner in the late 70s and early 80s. My fascination grew for this place where open-air public speaking, debates and discussions were allowed. Here, one could talk on any subject, as long as the police considered their speeches to be lawful. How I longed for this childhood dream of making a difference by getting powerful speeches across to become a reality. My hero was Martin Luther King, his speech *"I have a dream…"* it spoke to me and I felt every word. My coaching practice has helped me become more confident and I also know that when one creates a goal it needs to be:

Clear and concise

    Realistic

    Ecological

    As if now

    Timed

    End step – evidence procedure

My number one goal in 2011, was to be an accomplished public speaker in 2012. So I searched to find courses that would help me achieve this – I had put it out there and so the universe conspired to help me. This help come through a community meeting I was attending on behalf of the organization I was working for. I met a young lady who invited me to the local Toastmasters. My excitement grew as I felt one step closer to achieve my goal; the club members were warm, welcoming and did everything to make me feel comfortable. I heard some powerful speeches, and then I was asked if

The Change 2

I would make a two-minute speech on a newsworthy topic. I froze for few seconds, then took up the challenge. As I walked towards the stage my mind was blank, feeling anxious, my legs were so weak and I could faintly hear the audience rooting for me. The topic was about a local children school not performing a nativity play because the Board of Governors did not think it was politically correct. My two-minute speech was passionate and I delivered it with gusto. I got a standing ovation and also got the second highest score in the short speeches category. Wow, this was a first for me, thinking on my feet and having such an impact.

I joined Toastmasters International's club in Stanmore, UK, in December 2011. Toastmasters is a world leader in communication and personal leadership development. They have some 313,000 members worldwide and operate in 123 countries, and the investment is something like £60.00 for every six months (may vary in different countries). I was given a competent communication manual with a series of ten self-paced speaking assignments designed to instill a basic foundation in public speaking. My maiden speech/Ice-Breaker was a six-minute speech in January, 2012. On the day of my performance I was nervous all day, but what kept me going was the success of the two-minute speech. I remembered the feeling of a great sense of achievement and I kept visualizing that moment, the applause and excitement that I saturated myself in that moment. The toastmaster announced, "Our next speaker is Antonetta Fernandes, please give her a warm welcome as she makes her Ice-Breaker which is entitled…" I had not given the title of my speech to the toastmaster because I did not think it needed a title as I was going to talk about myself, but thinking on my feet again, I announced, *"Sixty in 6 minutes."* This created intrigue, mystery, and a whole lot of laughter. I will always remember the looks on the audience faces when I finished. It was priceless, and the evaluator comments were: *"great content, awesome story*

— with opening/ body/ closing, no a-hs, perfect grammar, delivered like a professional speaker. Improvements could be made by looking at all the audience rather than a few in the front." WOW! This was the day I will remember forever, it was a week after my 60th birthday in 2012. What caused the intrigue was I look about 40 years old. From then, I grew more confident with each speech. These are some of the comments during my time with Toastmasters International *"Quite challenging telling three stories & connecting to one theme, great delivery, passionate and a natural born speaker;" "Motivational Message from Miss Motivator;" "Diamond inspiration, and sparkling performance." "As Madame Toastmaster, Antonetta brought a new dimension of professionalism to an entertaining evening with her repertoire for compering."* With great reviews from fellow Toastmasters like *"outstanding performance;" "we saw you grow before our eyes;" "you are set for the world stage and tonight we were lucky to see a little glimpse of how great you really are."*

Since then, I have delivered many power-packed speeches, and one that stands out is a speech titled *"Aces of diamonds"* (which was written by Russell N. Conwell, and had been used in about 6000 of his speeches) given to a group of young entrepreneurs. This was my staged show. I dressed the part sparkling from head to toe. The music was Shirley Bassey's, *"Diamonds are Forever."* And the message was quite simple, "One need not look elsewhere for opportunity, achievement or fortune - the resources to achieve all good things are present in one's own back garden." I had finally achieved my goal for 2012, of being a good public speaker.

What next? I was approached by a singer/vocal coach to take up her Voice of Excellence Masterclass workshop. I met her at work and there was something special about her, and I felt a strong connection. At first, I thought what could I possibly learn, but I also know there is always something more you can learn. I am not complacent, and remembered this quote: *"To think creatively, we must be able to look afresh at what we normally take for granted,"* by George Keller. Although my Saturdays are for recuperating from running my own business and working for an organization, I felt the need to sign-up for the Voice of Excellence Masterclass workshops. I went in with an open mind, but by the end of the first workshop, I realized there was so much more to making your voice heard. Although I attended only three of the workshops, what learned was so priceless. It was the icing on a cake. Understanding the importance of voice warming-up and warming-down exercise, (I thought this was just singers, but how wrong was I - it is also about keeping your voice healthy) the breathing techniques on how to breathe and support your voice correctly, and body care - which covered types of foods to avoid, the importance of getting plenty of sleep, avoiding smoking or excessive coughing and throat clearing.

Wow, I felt the difference and so did my audience. And I was so grateful for the new learnings, I felt the need to explore with creating my own guided meditation/visualization programs. I would test these out on my coaching clients via Skype and face-to-face sessions. I got a mixed bag of reviews. So, yes, there is always something more to learn to perfect the technique.

At the end of October, 2014, I met a lady who I know will take me on to a different level of understanding. She gifted me a copy of her book *Super-Coherence: The 7th Sense*. What intrigued me were the questions on the back cover: *"A 100-watt light bulb and 100-watt laser. What is the difference?* **The laser is million times more powerful and effective. Humans mostly operate at 100-watt light bulb level.** *Would you like access to the laser level?"* My answer is yes and I have just starting applying the initial learning. The results are phenomenal and will share them once I finish reading the book and have attended her workshops, which are currently being finalized.

I wrote this chapter with you in mind. My story is about inspiring you and giving you tools and tips that you can apply in your own life to elevate the fear of public speaking. Here's to you finding your voice. As for me, I am now ready to perform Elizabeth Barrett-Browning, "How do I love thee, let me count the ways…" in all my regalia and Victorian costumes. It has been a great honor to share this with you, and a heartfelt thanks to the compilers of this book.

And finally, a few words from the book that is currently changing my life, by Thrity Engineer, which is a befitting place to finish. I have embraced change and you can see the results I have achieved. "When the winds of change reach gale force, it will be too late to start learning new tricks." So be the change you wish to see.

http://www.antonettafernandes.co.uk

www.afauthor.co.uk

www.mrsspeaker.co.uk

Facebook : Antonetta Fernandes Self-Esteem Life Coach

Twitter: https://twitter.com/Fabasia

Skype ID: annette6699

Email: antonetta@antonettafernandes.co.uk

The Change 2

Ellie K. Borden

A natural leader, entrepreneur, life and business coach, and a sought after keynote speaker, Ellie's goal is to help people from around the globe become the leaders they were born to be. After graduating from McGill University, she opened a successful record shop. Subsequently, her love of music led her to New York City, where she recorded music with world renowned artists like Swizz Beats, Just Blaze, Cool & Dre, Doug E. Fresh, Elephant Man, and more. After leaving the music industry to start a family, and inspired by motherhood, she hand-picked a research and development team to help create RawGoodies®, a naturally-sourced, positive living brand. In 2009, pursuing her passion to help others, she studied NLP and Feng Shui, and introduced the public to Blaze Your Trail - Life and Business Coaching. The Montreal Center for Anxiety and Depression recognized Ellie's stellar results in peak performance coaching, and she joined their "Dream Team" as their sole Life Coach/Personal Development Expert. Her passion for fashion flare, and her dedication to helping women push their limits and build their confidence, sparked the creation of Sexy Beast Lingerie. Ellie's vision is to teach others about the winning combination of both personal development and business training. And, by establishing the PowerCircle Women's Academy, Ellie is able to provide that winning recipe of success to women from all around the world.

CHOICE

It's Much More Powerful Than You May Think. *It's the KEY.*

By Ellie K. Borden

Even though it was a lifetime ago and I was only seven at the time, the event of that day remains a defining moment in my life.

I remember it being a calm and serene day when we walked into the restaurant. We sat. We ate. We made conversation. I felt all icky inside and a storm of anger was brewing.

And when we left I said to my mom, "Promise me something."

"Sure baby, what is it?"

"Don't make me see him again, but don't tell him I said it."

"I promise, if that's what you want."

This was a major turning point in how I interpreted my power as a child. My mother permitted me to have control, or a "say" in my own destiny through the choices presented to me. And that day I chose to never see my father again. And with that, we walked away from the suffering that came hand in hand with that relationship.

The purpose of this chapter is to help you internalize the following — you always have a CHOICE.

> "Everything can be taken from a man but one thing: the last of human freedoms - to choose one's attitude in any given set of circumstances, to choose one's own way."

> - Viktor E. Frankl

The ultimate human freedom is the power to choose. Do you believe you must change whom you are to get what you want? I don't! I believe you first must find your *true self* and your *true potential*. Then, you must optimize your program and upgrade your version to a better one. If you are not currently happy with what you have, or with the situation you're in… CHECK YOURSELF!

My mother's decision to leave the abusive relationship and stay strong in the face of fear, shame, and guilt, was a powerful choice that I, beyond a shadow of a doubt, believe in. Because of this decision, she changed the trajectory of our lives. For her, she reclaimed what was hers: self-love, self-empowerment, and self-respect. She found her true self, the self that did not give "permission" to anyone to perpetuate inappropriate behaviors. Hence, she had the freedom to pursue her true potential and her optimized self. For me, it taught me the most important lesson of my life: What we choose is how we live; that *every* situation calls for a choice; and that every circumstance requires boundaries. It taught me to push past my fears, to stretch beyond my comfort zone, to test my beliefs, and to keep pursuing my potential. It taught me courage to take a stand and to choose the unpopular and less conventional path, which in turn allowed me to unleash my deepest desires onto the world.

What is choice? Choice is an expression of autonomy. Choice plays a determining role in the direction and quality of a person's life. When people use choice, they empower themselves with thoughtful, calculated decisions about what they want to do in a given situation, and how they want to show up in the world. When you make choices that don't feel right, or when you just let things slide, you are not using your power to steer your life in your desired direction. You are simply riding the bus on a designated route. Acknowledge and understand the power of choice. Choice allows self-reflection and self-awareness. We can't change what we don't acknowledge or even notice. So by making choice imperative, we unlock possibilities that liberate us from the horrible feeling of being stuck and helpless. We remove the option of being the victim

Whatever you were raised to believe as a child is exactly how you will filter your experiences. If you had a cheery upbringing, filled with many memorable and happy moments, then your beliefs will likely support you in learning how to process information differently, in order to get different (and better!) outcomes. That belief system has everything to do with the choices you make. These choices turn into habits and behaviors that we adopt throughout our lives. For example, if your upbringing was dysfunctional, as a consequence, you may choose to drink excessively, manage to be late for meetings, or fall in love with the same persona over and over again. These are habits that are unique to you through conditioning. They become a part of your identity, but some of these patterns, the ones that don't serve you, are the ones you want to change. The good news is that the subconscious is built upon a cluster of habits. Fortunately, bad habits can be replaced with good ones: Habits that will serve you and those around you. If you want it badly enough, you will find a way; if you don't, then you will find an excuse.

Keep in mind the power of choice, and that all the choices you make throughout your day - good or bad - have a ripple effect. Imagine a young woman going out into the world with a chip on her shoulder, verbally knocking people down if they get in her way. That one harsh word she may say to you could cause your feelings to get hurt, and in turn, preoccupied by your emotions, you snap at your server at the restaurant, hence in turn, he or she delays your order - and on it goes - the ripple effect. Conversely, envision yourself waking up tomorrow with a different intention. You can go to bed tonight with the decision to carry yourself out into the world a little differently tomorrow. Maybe you'll decide to kiss your kids goodbye with a hug and an "I love you," instead of the usual, "Hurry up will ya? We're late!" Ahhh, now your ripple effect becomes a beaming light of positivity and appreciation, transporting inspirational vibes. Now your children go to school with a smile, full of joy and ready to conquer the day. In turn, the teacher is pleased at your children's behavior and compliments them as such. Now it's a healing light, an inclination for others to pay it forward, a caress of kindness, or even a friendly kick in the pants that reminds people to bring them out of despair. Why? Because you are modeling your belief that you are choosing happiness and fulfillment, always keeping your eyes on the prize.

Come along with me as we explore three major themes on the effects of choice and how the choices we make – or don't – play a major role in determining success or failure.

> "Our self-respect tracks our choices. Every time we act in harmony with our authentic self and our heart, we earn our respect. It is that simple. Every choice matters."
> – Dan Coppersmith

- Self-worth: Answer this, "how and with what do you define your worth?"

    You may have come from a dysfunctional family. You may have been abused, neglected, or constantly criticized. You may have been teased or bullied at school because you were different. Make no mistake here, as children, our emotional development is immature, and how these young minds internalize these experiences is significantly different from how they were intended.

    But regardless of what happened to us as children, now as adults, we can re-build our self-worth by believing in our abilities. Test your limits beyond your comfort zone and maintain a laser focus on positive outcomes. Our self-worth can be redefined by a collective of growth and success in our numerous roles, as opposed to defining our self-worth by one role. A classic example is of the woman who becomes a mom. The ambitious, sexy, and flirtatious woman, however she used to define herself, has now shifted her self-worth to being represented by her role as a mom only. She may now choose to ignore the need, or interest, for enhancement in other areas of her life. Or, what happens to a family man who defines his self-worth as the provider, when he loses his job. Similarly, what happens to you when the basis for your own self-worth is determined by the job you used to have? When your evaluation of yourself is based on the highs and lows of your career, the way you feel about yourself will fluctuate right along with your job status. This is unacceptable; it's half a life. Conformity is the death of individuality. You must embark on "identity decoding and re-shifting" to reprogram your self-worth. Approval of oneself has nothing to do with the calm or chaos outside of you. How you feel about yourself should not be tied to external forces.

When you perceive yourself as worthy of the best, then you make the choice to never settle for anything less than the best. You expect the best from yourself, from the man or woman you are dating, from your friends, etc. I had someone say to me that I have a great husband, and that I'M LUCKY. It's not about luck. It's about making sure that I was true to myself when choosing my partner. It's about attracting the right person, and choosing a partner who will support and compliment the unit that I belong to. For example, if you are a devout athlete and you chose a partner who prefers to join your daily run by following you in the car, you are not being true to yourself, because it will eventually develop resentment. Do not settle for anything less than what you are worth or strive to be.

> "You have been criticizing yourself for years, and it hasn't worked. Try approving of yourself and see what happens."
>
> –Louise L. Hay

2. Confidence – Do you have the confidence to make a decision - large or small, significant or insignificant? Does fear get in the way? Do you become anxious when confronted with a decision? Do you stay stuck where you are, then feel defeated as this wreaks total havoc on your self-worth? Do you start beating yourself up because you simply could not make up your mind? It gets even more complicated, doesn't it? Even worse, when you finally do make a decision, you have no faith in the choice you made. Do I marry him or walk away? Should I take

that vacation I can't really afford or stay home for the holidays? Eat that piece of cheesecake or read a book?

When you don't have confidence, making decisions can be overwhelming. You stay stuck in situations and relationships that are not ideal for you and fall into victim mentality. You don't trust yourself to make smart or appropriate choices. What if you make a bad decision and you end up unhappy, or hurting someone? Who wants to take responsibility for all that?

We are fortunate, as individuals to have the ability to choose. It is this ability that allows us to nourish our confidence. How? Make choices to eliminate the victim mentality; take accountability for your choices and actions; and choose to be the driver in your own life. You will soon discover you are more than capable than you gave yourself credit for. Once you have the proof that you can accomplish things entirely on your own, your comfort level in the face of adversity will increase your confidence to take on more, and to face challenges head on. When you improve your confidence, your anxiety levels decrease while you experience an increase in your ability to cope, thrive, and become unstoppable and resilient. Some choices may not be the right ones. Owning up to your poor choices, rather than blaming external factors, takes a certain amount of confidence. The confidence leaders are made of.

That said, want to or not, like it or not, whether you take the wheel and drive your life in the direction of your vision or stay stuck, you're still responsible! Whether you make a change or don't, you're still the one responsible for what your life is like. Reason being, you made the choice.

When you lack confidence and don't trust yourself enough to make choices, you abdicate all your power. Unwittingly, you end up with fewer choices to make, which is the opposite of the desired results you seek.

Catch yourself making a small decision and then another. Pay attention to all the choices you have in a day (what to wear, what time to leave for work, who to have lunch with, how you will behave with your kids, and what you will make for supper). All these mundane daily activities actually require choosing! Every time you claim ownership of having made a choice in any of these scenarios, you are validating yourself, and this validation over time should increase your confidence level. Try this and observe the change in yourself. Though subtle at the beginning, you will find, in time, you are more courageous when facing forks in the road.

A small tip to help you build on your confidence: Visualize in the present tense as if it is already a memory of a successful task, goal, etc. One theory states, the subconscious mind does not have an understanding of past or future, so by stating, "I will have money one day," it is meaningless to the subconscious. However, "I am a millionaire," is accessible to the subconscious. For example, if you know that in one month you will be interviewed for a coveted promotion within your company, and competing against other candidates, then visualize that you just have been hired for the position and all its perks. In other words, the 'act-as-if' mentality changes your confidence level tremendously.

Another helpful tip is to slowly shift your comfort zone, so that you can make small successful steps. Success reaffirms your confidence. I call it the "cliff hanger" - analogous to the game on The Price is Right, where the price has to be on point, or close to the right price, or the mountain climber falls off the cliff. Likewise, if you attempt to take on a huge task and fail, your confidence and self-worth is hindered. But if you go about it step by step, success has a higher probability, and with each successful outcome is a boost to your confidence.

3. Self-control is not only about battling with oneself whether to choose one thing or event over another. It's far more complex than we originally thought. It's about regulating your emotions. Not everyone has a high Emotional Intelligence (EI). People with higher EI are better at understanding their psychological state of mind. This can include managing stress effectively and being less likely to suffer from anxiety. Those with lower EI are more likely to externalize, for example they may say, "You're stressing me out!" Whereas, one with a high EI is more likely to take control of his or her emotions by resisting external factors, and by understanding that only he can choose to allow something or someone to stress him out. To achieve a healthy level of EI, you must implement techniques that allow you to regulate your emotions, and thus establish more control over your life and emotional state.

Four key techniques to support the development of a healthy EI are: Inner exploration for self-awareness; strategic planning for proper life-management; balance; and stress management.

Once a higher level of EI is achieved, then all other decisions and temptations in your life will be dealt with maturity, with focus, and with well-calculated decisions. You'll take control of your life and own your choices with no regrets. Along the way, you'll extract all the meaningful experiences that are the mortar of the building blocks of your wisdom. And with that comes higher self-esteem, self-worth, more confidence, better relationships, fewer bad habits (binge-eating, nail-biting, promiscuity), and so on. That is a powerful thing!

Life is not without it's struggles. The downs bring life-changing ups, and the ups put the downs in perspective. Dare to live! Wake up and ride the bull of life. Put your back into it! Sweat it out. Feel it. Internalize your power to endure struggle. If you are a man looking for his role in the world - dare to be the kind of man that reflects on his choices and redefines all the areas of his life. Maximize your potential in every area - not just in the traditional sense, or what society determines your role to be. If you are a woman - dare to be that woman that mirrors an Amazonian warrior with a clique of badass chicks with spears that you carved with your bare hands. Ready to take what's owed to you. We all have the birthright to establish our identity in a space of limitless potential.

But how does one take control and stay there? The answer is in an undying desire to be a person who is in charge of his or her own life; it is in the desperate need to be true to oneself, to achieve one's life goals. Desire is the driving force behind choice making.

A shift in perception can make all the difference in your experiences. If you regard every situation as an opportunity to choose, then you are essentially opening yourself to possibilities and other available options you might not have considered. With that said, can you not shift your reality to suddenly notice many more choices you thought were unavailable prior to your shift?

Show the world you're going to take life by storm, by making all the right choices to live your life on purpose and with purpose. Now is the time to blaze you trail!

"The pursuit of happiness is a matter of choice… it is a positive attitude we choose to express. It is not a gift delivered to our door each morning, nor does it come through the window. And it is certain that our circumstances are not the things that make us joyful. If we wait for them to get just right, we will never laugh again."

— Charles R. Swindoll

Contact info:

Ellie K. Borden   Founder, RawGoodiesB® - Blaze Your Trail - Sexy Beast Lingerie – PowerCircle
Main email: ellieborden@icloud.com

Main web: www.ellieborden.com

LinkedIn: https://www.linkedin.com/in/ellieborden

Web: www.rawgoodies.com

FB: www.facebook.com/RawGoodies.Shop

Twitter: https://twitter.com/RawGoodies

Web: www.blazeyourtrail.expert

FB: www.facebook.com/EllieBorden

Twitter: https://twitter.com/EllieBorden

Web: www.sexybeastlingerie.com

FB: www.facebook.com/SexyBeastBoutique

Twitter: https://twitter.com/LingeriePalace

Web: www.powercircleacademy.com

FB: www.facebook.com/POWERCIRCLEACADEMY

Twitter: https://twitter.com/PowerCircleAcad

Ashley Dais

COUCH TALK LIFE COACHING, LLC was created by Ashley in February, 2008. Ashley is a mother, Internationally Certified Alcohol and Drug Counselor, mental and emotional wellness life coach, speaker and author. She is dedicated and invested in each client to meet your different mental and emotional wellness needs and help with recovery and support through comprehensive addiction counseling.

Couch Talk started as a Life Coaching business, but as the need of struggle grew in the area of mental and emotional issues, Couch Talk focuses on mental and emotional wellness and addictions counseling. We specialize in the restructuring of thought process, helping refocus your life goals and emotional wellness, and restoring balance and healing to life. We utilize tools and techniques to make accurate assessments to ensure the best services are provided. If the assessment is beyond the scope of practice for Couch Talk, then appropriate referrals will be made to local agencies.

Understanding and Healing Emotional Pain

By Ashley Dais

Sometimes we feel ready to give up, to let go of everything we've worked for, because of overwhelming emotions and thoughts that leave us burnt-out, depressed, and anxious. Coming to understand this pain and learning to heal it, is a process that takes both time and conscious effort. There are certain steps that you need to take to resolve your emotional struggles and move on to the healing stage of your life.

The first step is to *recognize* the need for this journey and to *prepare* yourself for it. These things take mental preparation because it can be exhausting to actively address the emotions that cause you pain. You recognize and prepare by going through all the patterns of your life, the people in your life, your interpersonal relationships, your own actions and reactions in these situations, and the actions and reactions of others. After you process your life, past and present, you must acknowledge that you need to change the core thoughts that you have always used to cope with life, because they are no longer working - if indeed they ever worked at all! You don't realize how much you have been tormenting yourself with the kind of thought processes you are used to. They have damaged you, and it is time to give them up, throw in the towel, and stop the fight inside yourself!

It doesn't matter whether you've been abused from the inside, or whether you've had your heart or your spirit broken. When you have a goal and a plan of action, you can learn to release the ailments that are holding you down, and you can begin to rise toward inner peace. Usually this happens after you start changing your behavior, which is the next step in emotional healing. You must come to understand your own emotional responses by identifying the triggers that cause them, and then you need to question your own perception of each of those issues and identify the ways you could have responded differently. This takes practice, but with a conscious effort you can train your mind to make these changes.

After going through the preceding steps, you may be very tired - you may even be in physical pain - but don't give up yet! There is so much more in you. You may feel that you have nothing to offer, that your life isn't going anywhere, or that you no longer have the energy to try, but you only feel that way because your mind has taught you to think less, not more, of who you are on the inside. When you think this way, you create an emotional disconnect within yourself, which grows into pain that you never knew you could feel. After that, you have to put on a false face to show the world that you're happy, even though you have trouble facing your own pain. This pain could be situational or ongoing; the point is, it has been affecting your ability to live as you were meant to.

Another step toward healing your emotional pain is grieving. You may begin to feel frustrated and lonely because you have chosen to deal with your pain alone, because others don't understand you, or because you lost them in the transition process. These are normal feelings. You may also be stressed out and overwhelmed by feeling the same, day-in and day-out, while you are trying to figure out how to make your next move your best move. You are tired of making leaps of faith while still feeling that you're going nowhere, and you're ready to give up your dreams, your goals, even the bare hope that you'll ever be happy. Grieving is a process that lets you feel everything, good or bad, that's happening to you. The changes you're making, and your purging of the things that have happened to you, are important but traumatic events, and sometimes the mind has a hard time letting go. For example, when someone close to you dies, you go through a grieving process in which you accept that they are no longer a part of your daily life and you learn to move on without them. You need to do the same thing to let go of the distant and recent causes of your pain. Most people choose to not deal with this, or they deal with it in unhealthy ways, not really purging the problems from their minds and out of their lives. If you do this, it just causes the pain to manifest in other ways, hurting your personal and professional relationships, interfering with your ability to work, and affecting your overall mental and emotional health.

I can speak about this because I have been there; I have felt this way, more than once or twice. I have fallen into a slump that I thought I'd never get out of, but I did get out. Once I knew the reason that my dreams weren't coming to pass, my relationships weren't working, and my career wasn't going where I wanted it to, I was able to see a clearer path, and my dreams and my goals shifted to finding my life's purpose.

We often let our emotions get the best of us because we can't always control them. Emotions are a part of life, and they help us move toward our purpose in life. You may not have realized it, but every situation you find yourself in is preparing you for everything you will encounter afterward, and even your pain is turning you toward your purpose. The problem arises when you prolong or ignore your pain. You see, everyone has a purpose to fulfill, and no matter what your purpose is, whether raising children or teaching them, whether working as a janitor or as a CEO, you are put into each position in your life strategically, to groom you for that purpose. All those failed goals and failed relationships along the way taught you things, and with each of them, you had to take the time to listen to the lessons and learn them, rather than just wallowing in your misery over the circumstances you found yourself in. Each time, you gained a little more strength and endurance through this process, even though you haven't acknowledged it. You grew wiser and came to understand more things. Little did you know that you would be put to the test later, only to find that you already knew the answers, because life (God) had been preparing you all along.

We gripe and we complain about what happens to us, but we fail to recognize that the things we fail at, and the things that cause us pain and discomfort, are only there to open new doors for us and to grant us new opportunities. If you just remained where you were, you'd never reach any of those doors, let alone walk through them. Life is amazing in ways that we might never understand, but that all serve the purpose of your good and your destiny, wherever that may be.

Many people think that feelings should be pushed aside and ignored, like they aren't even part of the reality we live in. Of course, most people who do this do it to protect themselves from the past, the future, and even the present. The past, because they don't want to deal with the pain, loneliness, and disappointments they've already experienced. The future, because they don't believe their new experiences will be much different from their old ones. The present, because they can't go backward but don't know how to go forward.

Regardless of what has happened to you, you can't be afraid to feel the frustration, sadness, pain, and loneliness that life has thrown your way. Feeling these things is the only way to get past them, and I'm sorry that I can't tell you it will be easy, but it's very difficult to "just deal" with pain. Most of the time, these kinds of feeling go deeper than the surface. They're embedded so deep that they can be physically felt on the inside. This is indescribable to anyone who hasn't gone through trauma or through life changes that affected their emotional state tremendously. Nonetheless it is very real.

People may just tell you to get over your pain, or assure you that it will be okay on its own, but at the time, you don't want to hear anything of the sort. You need to grieve over the trauma you've experienced. This is a transition period for you, and if you don't let yourself grieve, you will never be able to escape those feelings, and you will never be able to move on with your life in a healthy way. Consciously or unconsciously, you will take your pain out on yourself and others in your personal and professional life. You have to be careful not to inflict such pain on your life for longer than necessary, or you will grow bitter.

You must take the time to understand the traumatic changes that have taken place in your life and that are taking place right now, because you must decide to be better than your circumstances even while you are still living in them.

It took me some time to come to terms with my own trauma because even as I was experiencing the present, the past would come back to me; the feelings I had experienced re-surfaced, causing me catastrophic internal pain. This time, I allowed myself to grieve over both traumatic experiences. It hurt like hell, but in the end it helped me heal. What got me through it was prayer and the realization that I was only going through a transition. During this transitional period, I admitted some things to myself, came to understand some things about myself, and realized what I wanted in my life and what I refused to accept in it. None of these things happened overnight, but change did come, and it's still coming. So never give up on the strength that you hold within you.

Another way we create emotional pain is by getting angry at ourselves for the emotions that we can't help but feel. However, it's not just any emotion that causes this anger; it is painful emotions that are attached to painful memories and experiences, past and present. The deepest parts of these emotions are tied directly to our hearts and souls, causing us such confusion that we just want to suppress and forget them so that we can move on. But the fact that we cannot forget them is what makes us so angry. This kind of anger causes us so much distress and such heartsickness that we either internalize it, turning it into depression, or release it outwardly in sarcasm, passive-aggressive behavior, or even actual verbal or physical aggression.

Anger at ourselves causes us to hurt ourselves in the most destructive of ways, from self-sabotage to alcohol, drugs, and indecent sexual behaviors. It makes us believe that we don't deserve any more than we have, and when a good thing comes around, we miss it because we're dwelling on our pain, our anger, and our past.

There are ways to move on. We have to begin by recognizing that we have the right to feel the way we do. Emotions of every kind are natural, and they should not be discounted at any time. We cannot help the way we feel, but we can help the way we respond to our feelings. It is natural to get upset with yourself if you feel that you've been made a fool of, or that you didn't live up to someone else's expectations. The problem is in getting stuck there. It takes concentration to make this stage into a stepping stone. Your heart will feel what it will feel, and your mind will try to make you believe it, but you can believe whatever you want, and you can train your mind to move past certain feelings in your heart.

Just remember these strategies:

- You should do this only when you are really stuck in a negative emotional state for a long time.

- Writing a list of the emotions you feel, and attaching events and experiences to each of them, can help you identify where your anger comes from.

- Affirmations are very effective if used daily or even (in extreme cases, but only you can decide this) multiple times a day.

- Making an effort to do things with yourself and for yourself is important to becoming friends with yourself again. Because you have been an enemy to yourself for so long, coming to be in love with yourself will take a lot of work, and the best way to start is by identifying yourself as a friend and liking yourself.

- Taking time out for yourself and acknowledging your feelings is one step toward identifying where you are and deciding where you want to be.

- Journaling about your experiences lets you both express your feelings about them and follow your progress in making the changes that will get you unstuck.

Use these strategies consistently to start feeling better about yourself and your life. Using only one will help you make some changes, but using all of them together will really let you progress and see significant changes. This will also lead to a change in your lifestyle.

It is harder some days than others to get through the emotional pain over what you've lost, the anguish over what you still have to deal with, and the torment of knowing that there's nothing you can do to make it go away today. But press through the hard days with prayer and silence; the good days in the future depend on how you handle the hard days of the present.

The more you talk about them, the more you'll convince yourself that it's too hard to overcome your feelings. Instead of speaking about the problem, then, move your thoughts straight to the solution, and you won't even have time to be in the problem. Remember, people can feed on negativity, and it can grow into your spirit and those of people around you if you don't remember that *this too, shall pass*. There will always be days when it's harder to get through the pain; it just depends on the events of your life and the thoughts that flash your experiences forward. It's up to you how you choose to handle these days.

I have learned that being still and moving only toward the solution, occupies my mind and keeps me from slipping into depression, hatred, and meanness. So, make sure that you work hardest on the days you feel the worst to keep consciously moving yourself toward feeling the way you want to feel. Remember to do these things:

- Evaluate what you want.
- Restructure your thought process.
- Refocus on the solutions.
- Restore balance to your days.

When you are going through emotional pain, consider taking these ten steps to help you through the process:

1. Slow down.

2. Stop jumping to conclusions.

3. Stop living for everyone else, and start focusing on yourself.

4. Learn what makes you happy.

5. Live for today and tomorrow, not for yesterday.

6. Remove yourself from negativity.

7. Ask who makes you feel this way, and when, where, and why they do.

8. Learn to tell people *no*.

9. Pour into yourself things and people of value

10. Be yourself, and learn to love yourself regardless of others.

These stepping stones will by no means cure your pain or remove you from where you're stuck, but they will start the healing process, and they will help keep you safe emotionally. You will need structure and commitment if you are to heal your pain. Take the time to understand your own needs, then decide how you can move forward.

Healing your emotional pain is not an easy task and you have to be willing to do the work. It is best if you have loved ones to support you through this process. However, not everyone has this option, so I highly recommend finding a counselor or a life coach to support you and to walk you through the transitions in a safe and healthy way. It sometimes seems easiest to do this sort of thing on your own, because you think you know yourself better than anyone else. The problem is that, with emotional pain, feelings and thoughts arise unexpectedly through the very healing process, which can be taking place at a very low point in your life, and they can bring you to an emotional halt. This means that you shut down and suppress, and you cease to make real changes or to heal. This is why you should take the time to draw up not just a plan of action, but also a plan of support, when you will be working through emotional pain.

To contact Ashley:

www.couchtalklife.com

couchtalklife@gmail.com

Caroline Gregory Pen

Caroline Gregory Pen became aware of her calling to reach out to others when she was 18 years old.

The road to fulfilling her life purpose was far from easy. It was fearful, painful and filled with anxiety, disappointments and loneliness. She got severely emotionally wounded at an early age and suffered from the consequences until her late twenties, until she finally found the way to change her self: her beliefs, her mindset, her patterns, her energy field, her vibes, her results in life.

Caroline believes that there was a purpose for her suffering. Life made her experience the change from darkness to light, from unconsciousness to consciousness, from emotional wounding to healing, for her to be able to help others who have experienced the same. Today Caroline guides others to switch from limiting beliefs to empowering beliefs and from victim vibes to Victory Vibes: a state of being, a consciousness, in which you have control over your life and start attracting love, joy, peace of mind, health and prosperity into your life.

Discover the Ultimate Formulae to Get what you want, the Easy way: Victory Vibes, you're ready for them, aren't you?

By Caroline Gregory Pen

Perhaps my Story will strike a chord in you; some of my experiences might sound familiar and resonate with you.

My sincere wish is that, if you're still in what seems to be a never ending dark tunnel out of which you can't sense nor remember your Light, you'll be inspired to take the right step towards a better life now.

How does one become a Magnet for disaster?

Smells. Petrifying smells. The scent of immediate danger.

Fear. Terrorizing fear. Emotions of anxiety and distress.

Screams. Horrible screams. Tearful pleas to stop.

Bruises. Dark bruises. Blood and broken bones. Sad reminders of endured pain.

It was snowing outside and our big gardens were covered by a cold blanket of ice and snow. It was on such an icy dark winter day that my deeply rooted trauma and emotional wounds found their origin.

That incident would mark the beginning of a long and painful, yet predestined and enlightening journey. A fifteen year long journey. Yes, it took me the whole of fifteen years to heal what had been broken in just a few....

Fifteen years to replace darkness with light; unconsciousness with consciousness; to raise my disaster Victim Vibes to success Victory Vibes: to free my energy field from the low consciousness of fear, anger and sadness and thus regain it's natural vibrancy – vibes of love, joy, inner peace and victory.

I know that this long journey was meant to be... A journey where I, eventually, after lots of pain and struggle, lost my Illusionary Self to the great joy of finding my True Self.

Before I found my True Self and could enjoy the Light that comes from this remembrance, I had to live in the darkness of believing I was someone else. Unloved. Unworthy. Unsupported. Incapable. Useless. Unwanted. Unsafe. Uncared for.

The tunnel of darkness is made of the wrong beliefs about who you truly are: all these misconceptions and limiting beliefs about Self that wrongly make you think you are the dirt that has been thrown at you, or that has uncontrollably grown in the depths of your Subconscious Mind.

The path to the Light is to get out of a limiting Mind-set. Shake off what limits you and lowers your sense of self-love, self-acceptance, self-esteem and self-confidence. Awaken the True You. You are a magnificent being. You are loved. You are supported. Regain your true power, your self-confidence, let go of the illusion of separation that overshadows the true magnificent beings that we all already are.

As I was fearfully running as fast as I could, barefoot, through the cold snow overlaying our big gardens, my mind froze.

'Was it real?'

'Did I just see what I saw?'

While my feet ran as fast as they could, my heart broke it's record of fast beating and my mind froze.

Shock. Trauma. The seed of a, from then on decennia long transformational Journey, had been planted, there and then. A journey through which I would evolve from believing being a Victim of life's unlucky circumstances, to awakening to the truth of who I really am: a powerful Victor. Yes, I can take control of my life. Yes, I can heal the wounds of my past. Yes, I can intentionally focus my inner powers to get what I want from life and, most importantly, yes, I am always safe and supported by life. And so are you, and so can You.

For the first time, I had just seen how my mother, after violently being punched in her face by my abusive stepfather, fell down. Horrified, feeling scared and powerless I instantly ran out of my home. Feeling the cold snow on my bare feet, I ran as fast as I could, across our big gardens, onto the street, towards my neighbor's home… for he, my neighbor, had a protective father at his home, someone I hoped I could bring back to mine, to protect my mother.

I had entered the dark tunnel, the imprisoning labyrinth. I was eleven years old then, and for a period of three years, my heart and mind were continuously bruised by wounds far more difficult to heal than those visible to the naked eye: invisible and hidden, how can one heal beliefs? How does one fix the damage of a troubled past: the emotional wounding and it's destructive consequences?

The pain didn't stop each time the dark colors of my mother's many bruises had once more faded. Neither when her broken arms had healed. My heart and mind had been wounded by all these experiences and it took me some fifteen years to turn them back to their original state, to their true colors...

It was not normal to have such a victim mind-set, filled with so much negative beliefs about myself, others, and life. It was not normal to believe I was weak and unsafe, it was not normal to believe I was unworthy of life's blessings and protection, it was not normal not to trust any men, nor life.

Sure, what I had experienced were the seeds hatching. It is because I lived all those horrible events that all those negative beliefs unconsciously grew in the depths of my Subconscious Mind. Limiting beliefs about myself, others, and life. My self-image became one in which I was a victim, fearful, unsafe, unlucky, unloved and unsupported. My view of the world became dark - one in which others are cruel and life is an unfair and dangerous place.

And as night follows day, the truth is that there is darkness and light here on earth.

What is not normal is to believe that only darkness will remain at reign. Anxiety. Loneliness. Hopelessness. To believe that the Sun will not rise or that its warmth is not for you, because you are not worthy, lovable, or good enough - this is abnormality. The truth is that love and light are, have been, and always will be within, and for everybody. The remembrance that this is our essence is called enlightenment.

Within yourself, you already have all you need to make the changes you want to make, the power to heal your wounds and limiting beliefs, as well as the power to attract what you want.

You will easily get what you want from life once you transform your energy field from Victim Vibes to Victory Vibes: once you release the energetic burden of the past, and instead, consciously embed your aura with the frequencies of what you want to attract into your life – wealth, health, success, love, joy, inner peace.

Once you discover how the law of attraction (LOA) works, as well as all the benevolent and supportive sources that are waiting for you to call upon them on the Other Side, you will be unstoppable. And quickly soar to unprecedented heights of whichever more of what you desire to get from life.

What if you could always enjoy the best of life's buffet?

We all undergo many changes during this lifetime. Some changes are unconscious. Didn't we all, without any conscious effort from ourselves, automatically change from being a sperm cell into being a fully grown adult body?

Throughout our lives, the organs in our body do not only transform, some of the beliefs in our Minds also change. The problem is, that similar to when our body starts an abnormal cell growth, our Minds can also be the victim of the birth of energy entities – beliefs – capable to destroy our lives. They too, just like cancer cells, if not removed on time, spread and create even more disasters. How? Because they emit a vibe, they send out a request! And the LOA always responds whether you ask for rotten tomato juice or your favorite drink… you ask and life brings!

Uncontrolled belief growth – not knowing what limiting beliefs you carry in your Subconscious Mind – is dangerous because the LOA will attract to you what you believe. Life will bring onto us the physical evidence of our beliefs, which reinforces those negative beliefs and make us wrongly believe that this is the truth.

So, the key to getting what you want from life is Change. Clean House! Remove the clutter in your Mind – out with the weeds – and in with the good seeds, the beliefs, energy entities, whose vibes will attract what you want to see grow in all areas of your life.

I know there are no coincidences in the Universe, and the fact that you are here now, to me, means you are Ready... Ready to release what is blocking you from awakening your True Self and living your dream life.

Not only does our body and belief system change in this lifetime, our level of consciousness does so, too. Life lessons are meant to make us evolve from prideful to humble, unforgiving to forgiving, unloving to loving, broke to abundant, unconscious to awoken. Lesson by lesson, our vibration transforms until our energy field returns to the high frequency of love, joy, peace and enlightenment – which is ultimately, everyone's journey.

Consciousness is easy to understand. Imagine the entire spectrum of negative to positive. Or, imagine a buffet. In the beginning, there is only some bread and water, and at the end, all your favorite foods. The LOA will always offer you what your energy field is made of - or what you resonate with. If you are a positive magnet, then this law will attract positive people and events towards you.

Life will give you the best of its buffet when you have completely cleaned your energy field from all unprocessed negative emotions and limiting beliefs. You will daily be presented with only bread and water when within yourself, you have not yet transformed your Victim Vibes into Victory Vibes, into Yummy Vibes… into a signal you sent out to the Universe saying: "Hey! I want the best of Life's buffet. And my way of telling you, dear LOA, is to already be that which I want to have, to be, and experience it… because this is how we place an order to get what we want to attract here on the planet Earth."

Your life is meant to be enjoyed. And the day you discover your true self, tune into your inner guidance; start to follow your dreams; trust this benevolent source that tries to guide you through your intuition; and perhaps, when you now also learn how to co-create with this Source - that day - your life story will rapidly reach new heights of fabulousness.

You will then not only be filled with abundance, success, love, joy and peace, you will, thanks to your vibes, easily and effortlessly attract even more of it every day.

Always remember, throughout your transformational journey, that there is a power that daily makes billions of cellular actions so you could change into who you are, now. It made you lose your baby teeth when the time was right.

This power has now brought you here. There are no coincidences. You are ready. Ready for the next level. Ready to release all that blocks you from making the changes you want to make, and from reaching your full potential.

There are unavoidable universal laws that affect the kind of results we get in life, like the LOA. Baby teeth grow, until they are replaced.

Yet, the sensational part of our human experience is that we are powerful co-creators! We can't control the weather, yet we can control the dark clouds crossing our mind – we can control our attitude in response to the dark clouds – what limiting beliefs come to obstruct the true brightness of who we truly are. Let's soar beyond those rainclouds, vibrate beyond limits, and there, enjoy our never ending warmth and light.

You can change what you believe, and so, what you attract. You can heal, empower and awaken. You can transform your energy field into Victory Vibes. Use the LOA in a way that changes Life into being like a friendly waiter that always gently brings you your orders, unconditionally, and effortlessly.

Be ready to revel in how supportive, lovable and generous Life is. Soon you'll notice how all which you find yummy is brought to you, easily and effortlessly.

Always Ready – Sic semper Paratis

My grandfather's name was Earl Carlton Wells, and as an American pilot in the Second World War, he was buried in the cemetery of Arlington, Washington, D.C. During the war, he was flying through French air space when his plane got hit; he pulled his parachute, fell into the waters, was rescued, and soon after, walked into a Belgian bar. This is when his eyes crossed the mesmerizing green eyes of my Belgian grandmother. Carlton was not only a war veteran - an American Victor - he is also an Earl. The following words are engraved on our family armor: *Sic Semper Paratis* which means *Always Ready*.

On my quest to change an essential life lesson I've learnt was to be *Always Ready*. Ready to remain Courageous, to keep going, to allow myself to trust in the goodness of life, to explore the possibility of a positive change to occur soon, to have faith, to dare step into the unknown; ready to protect my Mind from its most common enemies: procrastination, limiting beliefs, doubts and fears.

My expert team and I will guide you towards victorious changes, through every step of the way.

Get yourself a magical and an invincible armor: Victory Vibes. Vibes freed from the heavy burden of the past and its legacy of negative, sabotaging, fearful and doubtful beliefs it created in you; Vibes, an energy shield, that protects you from misfortune energies; Vibes, an aura, that works like a powerful magnet which attracts the best of life's buffet, and its delicacies in the form that you enjoy the most.

You are not alone, you have never been. Perhaps, just like the invisible warmth of the light that can't be sensed whilst you're feeling cold and afraid in the dark; perhaps you now remember that, even though it seemed like it would never end, however long the night, dawn will come. The Sun always rises again, and for you, the time is now.

What would happen if…. you avoid some of Life's worst Disaster Recipes?

I have so many years of successful practice at getting what I don't want from life, that I sometimes felt like a master chef, for disaster.

And in my online TV show, I will share some of my ultimate disaster recipes. It's 100% guaranteed that if you follow them, you'll NOT get the results you want. They won't allow you to make the changes you want to make; neither will they get you from where you are to where you want to be.

During my long and tedious training at the University of Life, what I wanted most, and failed most at, was simply L.O.V.E.

With the word 'L.O.V.E.' I mean Good Vibes: to be happy, simply. Not just on stage, also behind the curtains. Deep down, underneath the mask of constant happiness I wore in public, I was not happy. I didn't feel loved, safe, worthy, good enough, nor supported. I had no self-confidence, no self-esteem, no self-love.

My TV show will guide you in getting what you want from life. Getting what you want is easy. Explaining how to get it is the most difficult part. Why is this?

Because your mind now allows new insights to shed light on the right path to take. It surely leads to where not to go, yet are you, yet want to and will be, soon after you realize this here will do it for you, that which you want.

The key to get what you want is Change. More precisely, it is learning how to change Vibes - vibrations. Follow me, and discover how.

I have a question for you, don't I?

What would happen if you knew you could transform yourself into a magnet that effortlessly attracts what it wants onto itself? That would be quite awesome, wouldn't it?

What if I told you that you already are one - a magnet? And that everything that happens in your life is there because of the vibes you emit, probably unconsciously.

Imagine that changing what you get from life only requires changing what type of magnet you are – what kind of requests you make.

Now just take a moment and relax. Allow yourself to be calm. Take a deep breath, hold it… and breathe out.

Now ask yourself: is your life most often filled with:

- anger or lots of love?

- grief and sadness or lots of laughter and happiness?

- anxiety, doubts and fears or lots of inner calm and wellbeing?

Do you most often feel like a weak Victim or like a successful Victor? Do you believe that you are not good enough or did you already remember who you truly are? *Precious. Capable. Invincible.*

Do you often feel unloved and unsupported by life? Or have you already discovered you are a powerful co-creator. *Guided. Powerful. Loved.*

Do you often fail at getting what you want from life? Or has someone already taught you how you can be victorious in the attainment of all your goals. *Success.*

Watch my show. Discover what type of magnet you might currently be and what you can do to change your vibes, to change what you attract unto you.

Or get yourself already some Victory Vibes Self-Development Programs so you can even more quickly start attracting what you want now. More info on www.victoryvibes.com

May the Good Vibes be with You!

From Light with Love,

CG Pen

To contact Caroline:

www.victoryvibes.com

Facebook: www.facebook.com/VictoryVibes

Instagram: www.instagram.com/VictoryVibes

Twitter: www.twitter.com/VictoryVibes

Christa Bonnet

Christa's life philosophy is simple: *to Empower, to Inspire and to Make a Difference*. She fulfills a variety of roles including that of mother, business owner and consultant, author, coach, mentor, and PhD Student in Spiritual Intelligence and Spiritual Capital (SQ) in business. Christa is a specialist in Enterprise and Supplier Development in South Africa and focus on Social and Economic Innovation in terms of targeted procurement and localization strategies, methodologies, capacity building and implementation. She is also the Chief Executive Officer and founder of The Difference Makers, a non-profit-organization, which focuses on women and youth empowerment with entrepreneurs in South Africa.

Christa has surrendered to her calling to serve and to make a difference. She has embraced her life purpose as an awakener to raise consciousness in the business world. Christa has aligned everything she does with the focus on POWER OF WE, to connect fellow Difference Makers that manifest in her life. She has embraced who she is, her spiritual gifts and her powerful connection to the Creator. Christa is passionate about her calling to make a difference in Africa and to empowerment women in business. She has aligned her mind, heart and hands with this purpose.

Empower Yourself On The Journey Of Collaboration From 'Me' To 'We'

By Christa Bonnet

None of us can do everything alone – no one can. But when you are clear and kind and act with courage, somehow life works out, opportunities appear, synchronicity happens, and all that you have to do, is your individual part.

Cooperation is the call of the time. Each of us are called to share our gifts to make a real shift in the consciousness of the world at the present time. This requires that we cooperate to serve humanity. This is the ultimate task given to you at birth: to withdraw from the pull of ego, to let go of who you think you are, to tolerate the challenges along the way, to accept your destiny, to discern your path, and to decide how you will get to your destination. This task requires that you face your inner doubts, fears and insecurities, and that you share your gifts with others to serve humanity without any attachment to the outcome of your contribution towards change, or to the ownership of the task at hand. The main task given to you at birth is to set transformation in motion, so that the universe can respond by way of signals, synchronicity and opportunities to guide and support you to reach your destination.

We stand at a tipping point as a new consciousness is emerging throughout the world. World poverty is the direct result of a poverty of spiritual values, including our lack of compassion and care for our fellow brothers and sisters. Violence, in its various forms, comes from the frustration and anger felt by individuals who have lost respect for themselves and others. The task of turning the tide on this state of affairs is a matter of changing the hearts and minds of people, starting with our own. Although people have hearts, it is as if many are heartless. There is less and less mercy, less tolerance, and less compassion. People don't have the time to listen with love, and yet they have the time to speak harsh words.

People so easily say they want to change and that they want to make the world a better place to live in, but often the desire to change does not come from deep enough within. So, the question is, "Can you change yourself in a way that allows you to contribute to changing your community, your country and ultimately the world?" Here is the secret: The old patterns are not going to let go of us. We have to let go of them. If you want an easy method of self-transformation, one that brings results, consider self-realization. Self-realization leads to self-transformation and being empowered. The result is that whatever you need to do, is done with clarity, wisdom and love.

This enables you to come to grips with the rules of life and to value yourself so that you flow with everything that crosses your path in a more harmonious way. It is a simple truth of life that when the hearts and minds of people change, then the world will start to change for the better. Such an undertaking requires our cooperation. Cooperation calls us to serve at all times – selflessly, generously, and tirelessly. Cooperation is not about self-transformation alone; it is about the changes that will take place when enough of us start to live from our highest truth, serving together in unity and harmony. Cooperation is about the shift from a disempowered ME to an empowered WE.

Cooperation is about working together to achieve a collective goal or aim; it is about going beyond our own limited desires to serve humanity, which often requires courage and inner strength to make this happen. Cooperation is supported by the virtues of respect, honesty, harmony, and generosity. In its essence, cooperation is a virtue of the Soul and can be developed through the path of self-empowerment. Once the virtue of cooperation has been developed, the value of collaboration becomes part of your authentic self.

When everyone is pulling in different directions, each of us fail to recognize our own unique importance within society; then either conflict or competition occur. All of us have something unique to contribute to life, though often we are too caught up in the drama of life to notice or even appreciate this. When you see your own unique abilities, you more readily will see the specialties and uniqueness in others. True cooperation is the ability to help others and to allow them to help you. When we collaborate with other people, we all make progress. For whatever the differences among our nations, religions or traditions, we all want to belong, share and participate in communal responsibility to make a difference.

Collaboration combines our individual strengths for a shared purpose, where you can share your worth in a mutual effort to bring mutual benefit to humanity. This does not mean that you cannot strive with pure intentions to enrich yourself, provided that you use your wealth to enable others to also improve and empower themselves. Collaboration works with what we have, not battling with what we do not have. It is a synergy of individuals working together for a greater cause.

If you look at your fingers, you know that they are separate, yet they work together for mutual benefit. They do not compete or bring each other down. Each of the five fingers is different; they are each unique, and yet it is only when the five fingers work together that, whatever we put our hand to, becomes successful. Each finger has its own capability, but the combination of each finger's specialty together creates a greater force of power. Even if one finger is missing, the task cannot be accomplished with the same ease, as each finger has its own unique task to perform. The same applies to the world we live in; each of us represent a different finger with specific capabilities and specialties, and through practicing the art of collaboration, together WE form the hand of empowered Difference Makers.

In today's world, it is more common for people to come into competition with each other, to comment about each other, to correct and judge each other, and to be bystanders and commentators watching from the sidelines of what is wrong with this world. Some people feel that if they collaborate, they have earned a right to some type of reward. People forget that we all are just vessels of change who have been entrusted with gifts and specialties to make a difference together. A deep attachment to the self and to things (greed), inevitably cause a lack of collaboration. Such selfish feelings and attitudes cause people to become caged in their tiny selves, so that all experiences are filtered through the limited ME of the self.

The virtue of cooperation, as the foundation for collaboration, is easily misunderstood and underestimated. Cooperation is the interplay of tolerance, flexibility, accommodation, patience, respect and appreciation of our differences and uniqueness. It is not a soft and fuzzy virtue. It takes courage, inner strength and wisdom, to be a consistent and empowered Difference Maker. Cooperation enables you to accept diversity and to embrace unity. It is not about being a pushover or just accepting things - not at all - it is about allowing your inner self to become part of something bigger so that unity and change can happen through collaboration. This is the shift from 'ME' to 'WE.'

This shift ensures equanimity, empowerment, easiness, and enthusiasm for the journey and for the tasks at hand.

Collaboration provides the means to take the next step, no matter how small or how hard, and for those steps collectively to reach a pinnacle of change. Neither cooperation nor collaboration are bargaining games in which one person's success is achieved at the expense of another. It is based on mutual benefit in all human interactions. True cooperation shows kindness, mutual respect and accepts the differences in cultures, religions or opinions of others, while you maintain your individuality. It creates unity in teams working together based on a mutual trust and support. It encourages others to succeed coming from an integrated mind and heart with pure intentions.

The beauty of cooperation lies in its simplicity. The simplest way to cooperate is to use the energy of the mind to create vibrations of good wishes and feelings of pure intent when interacting with others. Practicing cooperation can be as simple as providing an explanation; giving love or support without expectations of getting something back from the interaction; listening with pure awareness; giving a blessing, kindness, smile, hug, or simply words of encouragement or an ear that listens to their story. It means that everyone you interact with receives something valuable from you as they leave your energy space lighter, easier, and filled with hope.

Collaboration starts with inner alignment of thoughts, feelings and attitudes so that cooperation with the world becomes effortless. When our internal and external worlds do not cooperate harmoniously, we exist in a state of disorientation, anxiety and stress. This creates separation and a lack of trust, which leads to an unwillingness to collaborate. All these blockages put holes in a task or goal. It is like a bucket containing holes; no matter how much water is poured in, it never gets full and cannot function as a bucket. Think of a task, relationship or goal as the bucket. If you do not plug those holes of doubt, no matter how much motivation, good words and new ideas you pour in, they will drain away without having any impact. When starting something new, ask yourself, *"Will everyone benefit or just me? Am I respecting people involved or am I using them for my own agenda?"* It is important to consider whether you are using another person to fill the gaps in your own needs, or whether you are appreciating the other person for who they are and for their contribution.

Cooperation is possible when there is easiness (being sincere and generous of spirit), and not heaviness (attachments to expectations) in relationships. When you embrace the virtue of cooperation, the ultimate goal changes towards collective achievement through collaboration, while you still excel in your individual capacity. Collaboration is everybody's responsibility, therefore, fundamental preparations are required to create internal support mechanisms, and the necessary attitude of detachment where nothing is taken personally on this journey. This enables you to look at others with an attitude of love and compassion, even after having being defamed, insulted or criticized by that person.

The way to contribute to change through collaboration, is to first empower yourself by understanding and knowing that you, and you alone, can transform your life. When your happiness is based on physical things, life becomes a struggle, because such physical things bring no lasting benefit. Having a purpose in life lights your inner fire and motivates you on your deepest level. This enables you to remain involved in everything, without being pulled down by anything. Being unclear about your values and purpose – in life, relationships, daily interactions, or within a group or organization – will make it difficult to collaborate with others on a collective purpose.

Real empowerment comes from deep within, from a place of knowing yourself. The more you know yourself, the closer you come to being able to express and live your truth without fear. An empowered person does not falter in the face of adversity, but faces challenges with courage. Empowered by your inner strength, you have the confidence to carry on and to take things in your stride, knowing that your consistency will eventually help you attain your goal. Empowerment is about taking full responsibility for your life and for what you create; to stand firmly in your own power and to make the right decisions. It asks that you look at any emotional patterns that are still active in your life that interfere with the process of becoming fully empowered. Empowerment impels you to take active, practical steps to achieve your goals and to banish all forms of procrastination. Being empowered gives you the faith, trust, and assurance that you have the ability to succeed in whatever you choose to do.

Self-empowerment is not an easy journey because its roots are buried deep within your being. Like the weeds in a garden, unless you get the roots out, they just keep growing back, therefore, changing only your thinking and emotions seldom lasts, as they have their roots seated in deep subconscious beliefs that you have assimilated at a young age. Changing your perceptions and decisions is not easy, as they too, are firmly rooted in your learned beliefs and recorded memories within your being. It has to come from within.

As you move from being disempowered to being empowered, your life will change dramatically. It will be as if you have taken a quantum leap and suddenly find yourself on the other side of life, where you always wanted to be. Living from a core of being empowered encourages you to live by your own principles and values. It is important to have clear boundaries while walking this path to stay unaffected by the opinions of others and the drama of life.

Empowerment is a personal choice. The journey of self-empowerment invites you to come out of hiding, to become more visible and not to be afraid to take the next step that life presents to you. It encourages you to live your life with passion and joy; to do what you love to do with enthusiasm, and to follow your refined intuition at all times. It does not mean a life without challenges and tests - to the contrary - it means that you handle them with more ease and wisdom coming from within, while you embrace everything in your life as a gift of grace.

By being empowered, you naturally collaborate with others because you want to share what you have learned and gained for yourself. You no longer think only in terms of yourself (the ME), but of humanity as an inter-connected whole (the WE). This is supported by your desire for change and unity on a much broader scale.

Unity, in this context, seeks an acceptance of all races, cultures, and religions; acknowledging that we are all inter-connected, it seeks to unite people through collaboration rather than divide them through competition. Unity accepts and respects the diversity of the global community; it recognizes that everyone has a unique contribution to make to the whole, and that this will be achieved when the barriers and prejudices between people are dissolved. Being empowered, you are able to go beyond the limits of color, race, and culture – and even beyond the differences of nature and personality.

Love and honesty supports you to collaborate with others to create unity based on one common goal: to serve humanity and to make a difference. Mastering the virtue of cooperation leads to living a life of authentic collaboration. When the awareness of the inter-connectedness and inter-dependence of all things begin to stir within your consciousness, the wish to know more about how to participate as an active member in the bigger family of Difference Makers grows stronger. This need to be of service then becomes an important focal point of your life. The focus is no longer on 'what is in it for ME?' but rather on a desire to play an active part in the creation and weaving of the tapestry of life to benefit the whole of humanity (the WE). When unity motivates your every thought and action, your life is filled with passionate purpose because you know you have a destiny to fulfill.

When you are spiritually empowered, you can literally feel spirit move through every area of your life; you know that you are in the flow of life, and that nothing can hold you back as you allow spirit to guide you step by step.

Imagine how it would be to take every step of your life with the connection of collaboration under your feet, in unity with fellow Difference Makers? You would never experience another moment of isolation because you will know that in every moment, you are always connected and actively participating in the co-creation of this beautiful web of life. Herman Melville said: *"We cannot only live for ourselves. A thousand fibers connects us with our fellow men; and among those fibers, as sympathetic threads, our actions run as causes, and they come back as effects."*

My invitation to you is to see what different choices you can make in your life, to bring change in the world you wish to see your children - and the children of friends and family - to live in over the next twenty to fifty years. I passionately believe that the future of the world lies in the hands of empowered people who are not afraid to dream a big dream; people unafraid to empower themselves; people with a deep desire to serve society with courage; people with an inner power that transforms, restores and reconciles; people who lead with humility, thought-leadership and vision. The world we live in cries out for universal love, peace, tolerance, harmony, collaboration and unity… and for you and me to take collective responsibility for the Change needed in the world.

The profound words of Nelson Mandela is a reminder that we are all members of one family, and that world transformation must come from empowered minds, open hearts, and collaborative hands. Madiba said, *"In the end, reconciliation is a spiritual process, which requires more than just a legal framework. It has to happen in the hearts and minds of people."* Commitment to this path will allow you to retrain your mind, to reconnect with your heart, so that your hands can serve humanity through collaboration to make a difference. All of this starts with self-empowerment, as we only can empower others once we have empowered and transformed ourselves from within.

Contact Information:

Christa Bonnet

Cell number: (+27) 82 600 9553

Email: christa@thedifferencemakers.co.za or christa@christabonnet.com

Website: www.christabonnet.com

Facebook: https://www.facebook.com/ChristaBonnet.DifferenceMaker

Twitter: https://twitter.com/christabonnet

Pinterest: www.pinterest.com/christabonnet

LinkedIn: https://www.linkedin.com/pub/christa-bonnet

The Change 2

Georgina Elliott

Originally a teacher of Performing Arts, Georgina started using coaching techniques in educational settings in the 1990's, to inspire young people to achieve their full potential. Retraining as a Life & Business Coach with NLP in 2011, she subsequently founded 'The London Confidence Coach.' Since then, she has worked with a wide range of professionals both across London and Internationally, helping them to gain the confidence and clarity to increase their aspirations and performance, in their work and/or personal lives. She has also written two confidence campaigns in the UK, linking confidence to physical well-being. She is an experienced workshop leader, running seminars and workshops on confidence related issues, such as: creating clearer, more honest spoken communication in the workplace; and building self-belief for women returning to work after having children. She has spoken on the theme of Confidence at a number of conferences and recently appeared on UK TV's 'A Different Kind of Woman,' as a studio guest, to give her views on how to let go of regrets. One of her forthcoming projects is working with the company Phoenix and the Wolf, to run her own six-day coaching retreats for change and greater empowerment, in the UK and Europe.

The Summit of Change

By Georgina Elliott

"Change your life today. Don't gamble on the future, act now without delay." - Simone de Beauvoir

Stuck up a Table Mountain

It is said that things come in threes.

Four years ago, three things happened to me that turned out to be significant catalysts in my own personal journey, each having the acute sensation of being on the precipice of the unknown.

The first took place outside the London school, where I had been working for the past few years running their Drama department. It was a Friday evening, everyone had left for the weekend and I had just submitted my letter of resignation. I left the building and very suddenly stopped in the courtyard in front of the main entrance. I watched the trees glistening in the early autumn, sun momentarily eclipsed by a rogue dark cloud, while I stood frozen, overcome by a strong feeling of huge uncertainty at what I had done. Do I go back and retrieve the letter, thus saving my reasonably paid, secure, yet exhausting job; or after over seventeen years in a profession that was beginning to drain me, do I honor my well laid plans to take a year off to change my life?

My heart said the latter, my head the former... and then quite disturbingly, my heart started to align with my head! After all the planning, raising of funds, sleepless nights, heated debates and justifications vocalized, I was finally on the road to freedom... applauded and envied by my colleagues and friends. The only problem was that at the very point of actually doing the deed, I realized the magnitude of what I was doing: the country in the depths of recession, and here's me, making a rash run for the unknown. Plus I really did like *some* aspects of my job!

Six months later, on a cliff-face at a somewhat higher altitude on the other side of the world, the path that lead away from the decision *not* to retrieve the letter, brought me to my second experience. I had arrived in the South American country of Venezuela after much cajoling by my travel pals, during a heady three months having the time of my life further down the continent. Traversing the vast plains and peaks of Patagonia to the Argentine capital of Buenos Aires - with its midsummer all-night alfresco bars and tantalizing toxicity of impromptu tango displays; topped off with the multi-sensory steamy madness of the Rio Carnival - anything seemed possible, including scaling the second highest table-top mountain in the world: the majestic Roirama!

Having spent the best part of two days trekking up a gradual incline in sweltering equatorial humidity, we embarked on the climb of the actual mountain itself: a path cut diagonally through rock from base camp to its summit of vast ethereal wilderness. After a morning of mostly clambering up sizable vertical boulders, the 'path' gave way for its final few hundred metrics to a steep waterfall, with our only option to climb it. I froze in horror, aware not only of the slippery, potentially treacherous surface, but moreover, the massive drop should I lose my footing. With my heart pounding and a strong feeling of nausea in the pit of my stomach, I found myself quite literally unable to proceed… my fellow trekkers long gone.

With the sound of water rushing at me tauntingly from above, beads of sweat dripped anxiously from my face. Our Guyanese guide appeared beside me grinning incongruously and attempted to talk me up this final ascent. *"Everyone else is at the top waiting for you. Being up there is a once in a lifetime experience… you can do it!"* At that point, I seriously doubted that. Who cared about the top? I could read 'The Lost World.' Surely Arthur Conan Doyle's colourful description of the otherworldly environment up there would be a reasonable compensation? I could see my friends' photos; I could train properly and COME BACK ANOTHER TIME! However, at almost three days walk back to our initial setting off point, I really didn't have a choice.

The patience, guidance and belief that our guide had in me very gradually got me back on that seemingly perilous path; my shakiness and uncertainty slowly giving way to increased self-confidence, so that by the time I was half way up, my fears were being pushed further to the back of my mind. And when I *finally* reached the top, the sheer elation and relief was incredible… almost superseding the incredible vista of surreal prehistoric rock formations and unique plant life that lay before me. I had truly landed in another world, with every second of the magic of being on that mountain (and sleeping in a cave) for the next two nights worth the initial terror that I had felt.

My third experience happened about eight months later, soon after I qualified as a coach. Having made it back down the mountain and home to the UK, to 'cane it' through my coaching diploma as quickly as possible, putting in long hours to finish it in five months so I could get going on setting up my own business, I just made the submission deadline by a matter of minutes. My sheer delight in achieving this in a relatively short period was however, disturbingly replaced by a feeling of dread, followed by a creeping, deadly feeling of inertia. The excitement and tremendous inspiration I had felt whilst laying my plans and then engaging with the course itself, had completely deserted me as I asked myself: *"How on earth do I put myself out there and get business?"*

Huge question marks presented themselves about my confidence and capability. My motivation spiraled downwards and for a short while I went into a sort of shutdown…distracting myself by doing everything and anything other than what I needed to do to get my business off the ground (including at times, nothing at all), while the blocks grew in size inside my head.

On each of these three occasions I had, *in theory*, been absolutely fine: *buzzing* in fact at the idea of leaving my secure job, having a daring mountain adventure, and starting my own business. At the route of each endeavor was the desire to do and achieve something I'd not done before, that I believed would bring me satisfaction and fulfillment. And yet once actually faced with the challenges, the classic response of *'fear of the unknown'* kicked in disturbingly at the crucial moment. And while I had made the plans and supposedly thought through each decision (possibly with the exception of letting my Brazilian partying get in the way of any necessary training for scaling table-top mountains), what I experienced right at the point of *doing* them very nearly had me bottle out altogether.

And now with hindsight, the sense of liberation at getting out of an increasingly demanding career that would have undoubtedly burned me out at some point during the remaining two decades until retirement; the phenomenal experience of being on the vast summit of a mountain amongst an ancient and isolated natural world; the regular dose of inspiration and excitement I now feel while running my coaching business and helping people make personal transformations, have each given me a tangible feeling of self-empowerment.

Possibly the very definition of 'empowerment' is to successfully come through a period of change and ultimately achieve something new in life that will bring a greater sense of personal satisfaction. It requires however, significant determination to leave our comfort zones, to conquer our fears and actually realize that often the reason we have this feeling of fear is because it's for something *worthwhile*. The more we want the change to happen, the higher the stakes. So high in fact, that we often persuade ourselves to believe that actually, we don't want the change to happen *that much*. It can be so much easier to ignore the 'worthwhile' bit and remain in a place that is more familiar, more predictable.

Except what's comfortable now may cease to be in the future, if its boundaries are not somehow pushed outward and redefined.

Five Steps to Making it to the Summit

1) Getting Beyond the Tree-line

The very start of the journey to desirable change so often starts with the confusing, uncertain experience of being in a haze: a feeling of disjointedness from the present, let alone the way forward. How many times do people say: *"I'm not happy with what I'm doing, but I really don't know what else is out there."* So many of us exist in this 'half life' of not really being satisfied or particularly motivated by current circumstances, and remaining in this state for perhaps years, until something jolts us awake making the need for change more immediate.

To see our way through this foggy existence is an enormous challenge. It will often require the support and guidance of another person, whether it be a supportive friend/family member, or a qualified coach who is trained to help bring about greater clarity and give space to explore options. It requires a depth of self-awareness about what isn't right now, and the possible *reasons* for this. It also brings a need for recognition of the *desired outcome,* plus the inevitable, not always comfortable shifts that will precede this.

This first step is in many ways, the hardest one. It is where an inward journey of self-evaluation needs to happen; a *readiness* for change and the desire to anticipate and face up to the undoubted stumbling blocks. It takes enormous bravery, overcome mainly by: a) a real desire to alter what is happening now, and b) a belief in a brighter future.

2) Visualising the Summit

"Come quickly, I am tasting stars!" - Dom Perignon

Once the fog has started to clear (which, with both persistence and seeking out the right people for support, it will), the second step is to consolidate what it is you're aiming for. What exactly is your goal? And what will the experience of achieving it be like? The more tangible the goal is - the more you have worked out how and why you want to achieve it - the more real it becomes. And very crucially, this in itself should inspire greater *motivation* to embark on the journey.

A couple of years ago, I coached a friend of mine who got a very late entry to run the London Marathon. Having taken part in nothing more than much shorter charity runs previously, she was apprehensive about her ability to run the necessary twenty-six plus miles; convinced in fact, that she would have to walk most of the way. Knowing her ability to be disciplined in other areas of her life, I suggested that it was completely possible that she could run the whole thing and set about helping her to achieve her desired end-result.

I set her a task to incorporate into her physical training regime. I asked her to visualize herself crossing the finishing line, having run the entire route. By first writing down in detail what she imagined this experience would be like - from the tree-lined, sand colored promenade of London's Mall, the delighted faces of her friends and family and the physical feeling of elation, to the audible cheers of the crowds and the sound of a champagne cork popping with its refreshing, zingy taste - I asked her to then 'pre-live' that experience in her imagination. The repeated act of really embedding this into her brain meant that whenever she thought about the event, any feelings of apprehension were replaced by a playing out of a successful and exciting outcome. She inwardly started to truly believe that finishing this race was possible. The more she believed, the more she trained; the upshot of which was, apart from a last minute irrational panic where she though she might collapse and no-one would know who she was, she actually ran the marathon in just over 4.5 hours… without stopping!

This relatively short-term goal definitely enabled our runner to dramatically push the boundaries of what she felt was possible, simply by being completely focused on the detail of her desired end-result and firmly aligning herself to the experience of achieving that. It's a technique that can be applied to almost any 'mountain' endeavor.

3) Planning (and taking) the Route

There are very few circumstances whereby achieving something worthwhile or undergoing significant change doesn't involve a good number of steps to get there. Of course these steps may be subject to change: life is by definition unpredictable and it's not always possible to know the exact route before you embark on it. However, anticipating and plotting the steps that are *likely* to be necessary in order to reach a goal not only provides greater knowledge of the journey that needs to be taken, but is more likely to help sustain the motivation needed to keep going. The recognition and celebration of every small step taken is enormously empowering in itself!

4) Overcoming the Obstacles

"Go back a little to leap further." John Clarke

And so we come to the perceived obstacles or blocks. We're all familiar with them: those real sticking points that erode our belief that a successful outcome to our journey is possible. The crucial thing is trying to distinguish between the real physical 'boulders' and what (more often than not), actually amounts to the barriers inside our heads. As a coach, I regularly work with people to help them deal with what they perceive to be stopping them from having the life or career they really want.

About a year ago, a woman whose confidence and sense of self worth was quite literally on the floor, came to me for support. Having been made recently redundant for the second time in eighteen months, she genuinely believed that having reached just her mid thirties, her career was over. The week before she left, she was told by her boss that she was *"shambolic, and disliked by her colleagues."* These not insignificant parting words had understandably left a painful psychological imprint, which further exacerbated the natural erosion of confidence that can come with losing a job.

Through lots of careful questioning and listening on my part, it took a while to enable her to unravel in her own mind, the underlying reasons for what had happened. She acknowledged that she had always prioritized getting the job done, as opposed to making an effort to communicate with co-workers on a social level. Although she had several close friends with whom she felt relaxed outside of work, there was a line that she had never felt she could cross with people in the workplace, for fear of appearing to be unprofessional.

As her self-awareness grew in terms of how she might be coming across to people (*"I'm realizing that although I'm a really focused, hard worker, people don't really warm to me: I think I'm actually stand-offish at work"*), we started to work on developing an understanding of the vital role that *rapport* plays in fostering good relationships with colleagues. Let's face it; most people prefer to work with others they can get along with, who help to make their working day more enjoyable! Together we explored: a) a number of techniques to develop her skills in this and b) the power of visualizing in detail the kind of job she really wanted. We called this her 'Golden Circle', which she would step in and out of to give it more 'physical' clarity.

Gradually, her confidence developed to such an extent that when the first possible interview came along (having worked with her to prioritize appearing 'warm, friendly and interested,' over 'competent and business-like'), she was immediately offered a role at a level *above* the one she had applied for, involving a considerable degree of (unplanned for) people management!

Since starting the job, her rapport skills have gone from strength to strength, thus transforming her work persona and bringing about all sorts of future career possibilities. Not only did we clear some significant blocks, she has furthermore since, recognized that the jobs she lost really weren't suitable for her at all!

Blocks can be a lack of self esteem, a clinging on to past events, a belief that time/circumstances/finance/ability is lacking, an imprint left by negative things others have said about you; which in turn cause a lack of motivation or stamina and a feeling that it's so much easier to give up. Whatever your blocks are, they can be effectively broken down by building a greater resilience and belief in yourself. Here are a few essential pointers to help achieve this:

- Stop allowing negative past events to hold you back. Try and stay firmly rooted in the present and focused on what you want from the future.

- Ignore the critics! Surround yourself instead with positive people.

- Be nice to yourself; and that includes banishing any negative 'inner' voices.

- Regularly remind yourself of what you already have in your life that's good... this is your foundation!

- Avoid comparing yourself to others. (Athletes close to the finishing line rarely look at each other. If they did they'd fall over.)

- Work at being *clear* about what you want.

- Recognize any steps backwards as an inevitable part of the learning process.

5) The Final Ascent.

"You will face your greatest opposition when you are closest to your biggest miracle." - Shannon L Alder

Often referred to as the 'Roof of Africa,' Kilimanjaro is the highest free-standing mountain on Earth, and owing to its steep ascent in altitude, considered one of the toughest to climb. With only 40% who attempt it actually reaching the summit, it has eluded some of the most agile climbers, otherwise extremely fit individuals who have trained for months only to fall at the final hurdle: the arduous midnight ascent to reach Uhuru Peak for sunrise.

I know a number of people who have embarked on the journey up this mountain: in some cases *just about* making it. One friend described this final stage of the route as *"one of the most painful experiences of my life. I was literally dragging myself up in gale force winds and freezing icy sleet. I felt incredibly sick and on the point of collapse, unable to walk a few paces at a time before stopping to recover. I'm not sure how I eventually made it; except I knew I had no choice. I hadn't come this far for nothing."*

Getting over the final hurdle means stamina, willpower and sustained motivation. It requires tenacity and patience and an enormous amount of holding your nerve. The need to focus, stay calm and not over-think the potential difficulties is paramount. Take it *"poly poly"* - one step at a time, is the advice of the Kichagga speaking porters who guide tens of thousands up Kilimanjaro every year.

So with the mountain as a powerful metaphor for the journey towards change, try not to dwell on the altitude as you proceed further up the path. And never, ever forget just how far you've come.

Contact details:

Web: www.thelondonconfidencecoach.com

Email: georgina@thelondonconfidencecoach.com

Phone: (00 44) 07973 721738

Jan Haldane

Jan Haldane is a bestselling author, international speaker, empowerment coach and relationship expert. She helps people live their truth with passion, power and presence. Based in Auckland, New Zealand, she has a large global following. As a coach, it is Jan's job to raise your awareness and facilitate you to live the life you want. Her coaching style blends conventional coaching and spiritual principles to move you forward to emotional well-being, success and happiness faster than conventional coaching alone.

By incorporating spiritual theories and quantum physics, Jan works with mind, body and spirit to achieve the best possible outcome for her clients. According to Jan's philosophy, you are not your story. Nor are you a character in someone else's story. You can change your story and you can change your life. The wisdom is within you.

Jan holds a Bachelor of Education degree and an Adult Teaching certification. She has Advanced Life Coaching certification, training in Strategic Intervention Coaching from Tony Robbins and Cloe Madanes, and has been certified as an Angel Intuitive and Past Life Therapist by Doreen Virtue PhD.

If I Can Heal My Heart, So Can You

By Jan Haldane

How do you mend a broken heart? A loving heart that's been broken multiple times by the same person. What does it take to restore belief in yourself and confidence that you can find a healthy love again in the future?

These are some of the questions I asked myself when my relationship with the man I believed was my soul mate, finally ended. My self-esteem was in my boots, and I struggled to believe in myself as a woman, mother and coach.

How could someone who had told me he would do anything to get me back just a few months before, and spoke positively about marriage, now have a multitude of petty reasons why our relationship would never work? It made no sense to me whatsoever. I spent weeks trying to understand his reasoning, until one day it dawned on me that it wasn't about me making sense of anything. It was about him and his fears – most specifically, his fear of commitment. These fears had literally killed our relationship and there was nothing I could do to change that. No matter how many hoops I jumped through, and how much I twisted myself into a human pretzel, I couldn't compete with the fears from his past. Fear is the opposite of love. No healthy relationship can grow from a place of fear. Fear is toxic, slowly poisoning the relationship as surely as weed-killer poisons plants.

Something had to change, that was certain. I couldn't go on beating myself up for being myself. Was I really unlovable because I disliked loud, thumping rock music and went to bed before midnight? Did yelling at my 18-year-old daughter for getting me out of bed to pick up a dead mouse in the dining room while she had drinks with her friends make me the mother from hell? In his eyes, I couldn't be trusted to live in the same house as him and his children. The really strange thing was, nothing had changed. I'd never liked loud rock music, late nights or disrespect from my children. I realized the only person I could change was me. In that instant I made a commitment to myself to use all my life experience, wisdom, professional coach training and spiritual knowledge to challenge the belief that I wasn't enough.

Here's the thing. You can leave any relationship you choose, but you can never leave yourself. Your relationship with yourself is the most important human relationship that you have. The quality of your relationship with yourself, or your self-esteem, underpins the functionality of all aspects of your life, because life is all about relationships, particularly for women. The belief that I wasn't enough was beginning to impact my professional life too. Who was I to help others when I couldn't help myself? How could I stop replaying the critical video and audio in my mind that reinforced daily that I was to blame, that I was somehow fatally flawed?

Now I look back and wonder how a successful 50-something professional woman could have become disempowered to this extent. Why had I given my power away? Why did I automatically feel I was to blame? Was it really to do with this relationship, or did this shame go back to my childhood? It's truly amazing how emotional baggage follows us through life. It's one of the first things I encourage my clients to work through, and I really believed I'd worked through my old stuff from an emotionally abusive childhood, but it seemed that I hadn't after all.

To really begin the healing process, I needed to challenge the subconscious thoughts that I still carried from childhood, thoughts that nothing I did was enough and that I must be automatically to blame for anything that went wrong. Intellectually I knew this was untrue, but a little gremlin kept nagging at me that maybe there was something wrong with me, like my mother used to tell me. It's interesting that despite a great education, numerous business and professional successes, friends and colleagues who love and respect me, and two amazing adult children, I still carried this old limiting belief.

From early childhood, we are bombarded by messages that make us doubt ourselves and our abilities. It's quite amazing how someone's throwaway remark can impact our entire life. That is, if we let it, if we don't challenge the validity of the original remark and the person who made it. Our still-developing child-minds internalize the messages we receive from authority figures in our life. In our innocence, we believe that parents, teachers, clergy, youth leaders and other adults must be right, by virtue of the fact that they're adults. So whether or not these adults have the knowledge or expertise to be credible judges, we still believe them.

Soon the years pass and we shed our childish ways, but not the beliefs imprinted on our minds. However, now we look at life with an adult mind ourselves. We are now authority figures in our own right. If we don't drill down to uncover and challenge our limiting beliefs ourselves, someone else will. And that someone will be in a relationship with you, because our relationships act as mirrors of what is actually embedded in our subconscious minds. Some relationships are positive mirrors and some are very dark mirrors. Whichever sort they are, they are reflecting your own thinking. Most importantly, they are reflecting how much, or how little, you love and approve of yourself.

Clearly, I had more work to do on releasing the childhood belief that I was not enough before it could affect any new relationship I went into. This kind of limiting belief has an impact not only on romantic relationships, but on everything that you do. Was I limiting business opportunities subconsciously? Was I somehow secretly sabotaging my professional life? It was time to take positive action. Calling on my training and the huge amount of professional reading I've done over the years, I created the Thought Release Tool, a series of powerful questions designed to identify and release negative and limiting beliefs.

1. What do you believe about men/women and relationships?

2. What do you believe about your worth in the world?

3. What experience/s prompted this?

4. Is this absolutely, 100 percent true, with no exceptions?

5. How could you reframe this belief?

6. How has this thought served/protected you positively in the past?

7. How does this thought hold you back from finding love now?

8. How is this thought now limiting your success in other areas of your life?

9. Who would I be without the thought?

While it was very difficult to confront and list these beliefs and acknowledge, challenge and reframe them, it was also very liberating. I felt able to lay down my burdens for the first time in my adult life. I felt infinitely lighter and freer of spirit. It was almost as if I'd just taken an enormous pack filled with rocks from my back. I wanted to dance around the living room.

Working with this tool finally made me understand how I had created my thoughts, which in turn had created my intentions, which ultimately had created my reality. Essentially, we are what we think. Our thoughts affect our body and our spirit. They can attract or repel love, success and abundance. Thoughts can heal us or make us ill.

There is no doubt that what you are thinking can affect your body in many ways. At that point in my life, not only was my mind in turmoil, my body had tightened up, especially on my left side. As the right side of my body began to compensate for this, I began to experience a lot of pain while walking. The combination of emotional and physical pain was now limiting my life by literally making each step I took painful. Simple things like walking around the supermarket were draining and tiring. Metaphysically speaking, I was manifesting this physical condition in response to my fear of moving forward on my own.

I've always been a very proactive and self-motivated person and I was very unhappy about the condition I was in. It was a very important part of my healing to understand how I'd ended up in this painful state. Dealing with the symptoms alone simply wasn't enough. I hadn't had a recent physical injury that had caused all this pain, so what was causing it? I knew the answers weren't to be found in mainstream medicine, so I decided to approach my healing holistically. After all, I was experiencing pain in my mind, body and spirit.

I couldn't leave working on my body until I'd worked on my thinking or my spiritual connection; it gave me daily reminders in the form of pain, that I needed to address what was going on. It was straight after the breakup that my body reacted to my emotional pain by locking up. In fact, I can pinpoint the time it happened. I was sitting at my desk at a charity that I work for, mulling over how someone could want to marry me, and a few weeks later say he still loved me but couldn't live with me for the petty reasons I mentioned earlier, when I felt I was literally being stabbed in the back by a knife. It was unbelievably painful.

Choosing to work with a chiropractor who specialized in Network Spinal Analysis (NSA) and Somato Respiratory Integration (SRI) was the best thing I could do for my body. Years before, I'd had an experience with a chiropractor who adjusted my back in a very rough manner, so when I met someone who could help me using a gentle touch, I was incredibly excited. Through gentle precise touch to the spine, NSA cues the brain to begin healing the body, while SRI reconnects a person's breath, touch, focused movement and attention, allowing them to experience the body more fully, and instantly shifting their state of consciousness to one that supports trust for the body-mind and their life experience.

Slowly, I regained confidence in my own ability to heal. The pain was there less and I could gradually go back to doing the things I enjoyed, like walking the dog in the park or taking solitary walks on the beach to chill out from city life. At long last, I began to feel like I was getting back to my old self. I had confidence that my body had the power to heal itself, and had a stronger understanding of how the power of the mind creates both our emotional and physical reality. If you are in physical pain or are unwell, stop and think about the body/mind link. Ask yourself:

1. What is happening or has happened in your life to cause your body to feel this way?
2. What can you do yourself to heal this condition?
3. Who can help you with this?
4. What is the cost of not seeking healing?
5. Where are you allowing limiting beliefs about your own self-worth to sabotage your health and wellbeing?

If you are in the habit of putting everyone else's needs before your own, it can be hard to believe that you deserve to spend time and money on your own health. Let me tell you, you are awesome and you absolutely deserve to be healthy, happy and whole. And before you think, "I couldn't be so selfish," stop for a moment and consider how much your compromised health could negatively affect the people who love you and count on you to have their backs - always. You are important, you matter and you are worth it. Your health and wellbeing are of paramount importance and you are capable of healing your heart, your emotions and your body. It's a matter of trusting your body's wisdom and believing that you deserve to be healed.

Perhaps the most powerful, and certainly the most comforting part of my holistic healing practice, was reconnecting with my spirituality, which I had neglected for many years. During a very difficult period of my marriage when my youngest child was a baby, I had developed my intuitive abilities to a professional level in the face of extreme disapproval from my ex-husband. On top of his negativity, I became scared of my own intuitive abilities. I had the gift, but wasn't ready to step into my own power. It was far easier to conform to my husband's wishes and devote my life to him and the children. While I put away my tarot cards and books for the meantime, I always knew it was something I would return to when the time was right.

They say when the student is ready, the teacher will appear. And so it was that I found myself on a plane bound for Brisbane, Australia, where I was meeting up with a colleague from coach school to attend Doreen Virtue's Angel Intuitive course. At this course, I found the missing link to reconnect me with my spirituality. I saw the potential of the gentle but powerful energy of the angels to heal my pain. Expanding on this, I saw how I could help others to heal their pain, too. I felt incredibly blessed to be able to learn from Doreen, who has simplified the study of angels so we can all understand how to make the connection to the angelic realm, and how to work with angel oracle cards and angel tarot cards.

One of the simplest but most effective tools in my healing was listening to Doreen's chakra-balancing meditations every morning and evening prior to going to Australia. From these meditations, I came to believe that I was loved with a greater love than is found here on the planet. This was a huge step forward - to think that I didn't need a partner to feel loved. It was given to me freely without any conditions attached. I felt extremely empowered and deeply nurtured. I could be myself, warts and all. I didn't have to worry about not being enough, because I was loved and accepted by God.

Learning how to connect with the angels changed my life and changed the direction my business was heading in. I realized how much I'd suppressed my spiritual side because I needed to be seen as a serious coach. The truth was, I could pick up a lot of information that would be helpful for my clients, but there was no way that I could relay this to them without admitting that I was getting information from above. The old fears of being judged and considered 'woo woo' were holding me back again. I knew that this was the time to truly step into my power, both for my own healing and for the healing I could offer others.

I rebranded my business, started letting people know that I worked with Archangel Michael, and the clients began to appear. My fear of losing business and credibility proved to be unfounded, as people sought me out to help them gain a new perspective on their lives with the help of divine direction. Gradually, some clients who were initially skeptical, also wanted to try out the spiritual side, and were amazed at how accurate and timely the information they received was.

Meanwhile, working with the gentle energy of the angels to heal myself and help others was making a huge difference in my life. I was feeling more peaceful than I had in many years, but there was still something that bothered me. Why did I still have this strong heart connection with this particular man, above all others I had met in my life? I needed to understand this link. How could I make sense of this, and finally let go of his presence in my mind? To move forward, I needed to give him notice on his long-term tenancy in my thoughts. Sure enough, when I asked the Universe, "What would it take to remove this guy from my day-to-day thinking?" I was given the tools.

When you ask the Universe for help, you will get it. But it may be in a different manner than expected. I happened to be on Twitter one day and saw that Hay House was running an "I Can Do It" weekend in Sydney, Australia. The line-up of speakers was truly inspirational, so without hesitation, I booked my flights and accommodation. The final speaker of the weekend was Denise Linn. She was talking about past-life regression and she actually regressed the whole auditorium of the Sydney Convention Centre. In this regression, I asked to be taken back into a past life with my former partner. In that lifetime, I was his wife and he allowed me to be murdered. One of the things that bothered me in this lifetime was that he never had my back! Clearly in this lifetime we were trying to balance the karma from that lifetime, and that's why the connection was so strong. This is so with karmic relationships, which are notoriously emotionally fraught.

On returning to New Zealand, I completed Doreen Virtue's Past Life Healer Course to learn more about how knowledge of our past lives can help us heal emotional pain, physical pain and phobias in the here and now. I regressed myself back into a life where my ex-partner was my son who I had very little time for. This made a lot of sense to me, as I'd often felt like a mother to him rather than a partner. As I finally forgave myself for that lifetime, and him for the other lifetime, the karma was resolved. I woke up the next morning and the emotional pain and attachment were gone.

We are now the best of friends who will always look out for each other. Now that the karma is resolved, we are free to have a pain-free relationship. If I can heal my heart, you can too. If the pain is hanging on, try something else. I wish you all the happiness in the world.

www.janhaldane.com

jan@janhaldane.com

www.facebook.com/janhaldane

twitter @coachjanhaldane

The Change 2

Lindsay J. Hallead

Lindsay J. Hallead has a wide range of experience and education that she brings to the table. She holds a Master's Degree in Communication with an emphasis in education from Spring Arbor University. She is also a Certified Life Coach with practice areas in women's issues, empowerment and self-improvement, personal and professional growth. Lindsay currently works for a worldwide non-profit agency as the self-sufficiency case manager and social services worker. She has implemented a self-sufficiency program in their extension office that promotes personal and professional growth, goal setting and implementation, and self-improvement. She has a loving husband and three amazing sons of which is whom she dedicates this chapter to. In her spare time she enjoys running 5K and 10K races, writing, journaling and travel.

When to Say Yes, How to Say No

By Lindsay Hallead

I'd like to start this chapter off with a quote that has helped me through many of my own times in need:

> "Self-care is not selfish. You cannot serve from an empty vessel." - Unknown

So, let's take a tour through boundaries and self-care. The first thing we need to know is what a boundary actually is: it is an invisible and dividing line that serves to protect and take care of us both physically and emotionally. It helps us to understand our needs and know what our limits are. Moreover, it helps us develop and maintain healthy relationships. Without boundaries, we wouldn't know where we are in relation to others; our interactions with each other would be chaotic and out of control.

Are You Setting Boundaries?

One important aspect of your self-care involves setting boundaries. Boundaries are basically rules or guidelines for what you need to have in place for you to be at your best - physically, mentally, emotionally, and spiritually.

Not sure if you need to take a look at the boundaries that you are setting, or not setting?

You might want to look at them if you:

- Have that vague sense you could be doing something more productive or healthy;

- Feel annoyed or resentful when you just said yes to something you know you will enjoy for the moment, but also know isn't going to benefit you in any way;

- Know that you are going to be exhausted because you just promised away time you had planned to use to take a break;

- Wish that the energy you are using for taking care of other people was also being used to take better care of yourself.

To some people, setting boundaries may be a challenging concept to implement in their lives due to common myths and negative connotations of the idea. Some may view setting boundaries as a selfish, rebellious, or disobedient act. Others, when contemplating on setting boundaries, may have feelings of guilt, or worries about how they might hurt others or be hurt by others as a result.

Setting boundaries is a skill that doesn't come naturally, but is developed over time through education and practice. This concept needs to be nurtured and practiced for us to be good at it. There are many ways for establishing appropriate boundaries.

Be aware of your feelings and body sensations. How do you feel when engaging with a particular person? Pay attention to any uncomfortable or feelings of discontent. Ask yourself, what is causing this discomfort? What is it about this comment or request from the person that is bothering you? For people who cannot immediately identify their feelings, it may be helpful to pay attention to any physical signs, such as headaches, stomach aches, or changes in body heat.

Be honest with your feelings. When growing up, you may have been told that showing emotions is a sign of weakness, and therefore, little by little, learned to bottle up emotions - sometimes to the point that you may not even know how you feel anymore. However, recognizing and being honest about your feelings is an important prerequisite in learning to set boundaries. There are no right or wrong feelings - they are just there. List these feelings instead of interpreting how you "should" feel.

Assert yourself. Communicate in a gentle, yet direct and firm manner. Yes, you can be gentle in your voice, yet firmly communicate your feelings and stand up for yourself. At times, you may have to be direct with certain people, more than you do with others. To be assertive in your communication, use a sentence like this: "I feel (express and name your emotions), when you (describe the behavior that bothers you), and I would like (state the specific behaviors you would like to see from the other person)."

Give yourself permission. Honor your feelings and give yourself permission to say no. It is an important step of self-care. Sometimes, you want to set boundaries but don't want to just say no: you can propose alternative options. For example, you can say something like - "I cannot help you with (their request) right now, but I am free in two hours (be specific with an available time). Would you like me to help you then?" Remember, you have to be comfortable with whatever options you provide. If an uncomfortable feeling still arises, it remains perfectly fine to just say NO. Don't feel obligated to give reasons for your response.

Know that you have a choice. As an American philosopher and psychologist, William James, put it, "When you have to make a choice and don't make it, that is in itself a choice." So, yes, it is your choice and right to verbalize and set the kind of boundaries you want with another person. At the same time, it is another person's choice whether or not, or to what degree, they want to respect these boundaries. Your choice then is to decide how much physical or emotional distance you want to keep between you and that person based on their response.

Learn to Reach Out. As humans, we cannot live alone: we all need help or support at some point in our lives. Allow yourself to say yes when others volunteer to help, or ask you if you need anything. This does not indicate a sign of weakness. It shows that there is a mutual trust between you and the person offering help. Therefore, it is important to reach out to someone with whom you trust and feel safe. When help is received, allow yourself to say thank you instead of apologizing for needing help.

It took me years to dispose of the habit of saying yes automatically when someone asked me for (or to do) something. So often had that single syllable fallen from my tongue, that I would often agree to things before people had even asked me. In time, I realized that I had spoiled the people around me to the point that they assumed I owed them an agreement, no matter how inconvenient and unreasonable their request was. Many times, if I was unable to concede, they would be agitated and annoyed - and I would feel guilty. To this day, I find that when I tell someone no, even a stranger, they seem surprised, almost offended, at my nerve.

And perhaps it is nerve. The fact that saying "yes" all the time got on my very last one, and kept me on edge. I would say yes because, as a self-described superwoman, it was the only word I knew to say. I would say yes because I was flattered at the request(s), anxious to please other people, and I was focused on making other people happy. I would say yes because it felt like the right thing to do, the polite reply to any well-intentioned question, and evidence that I was a good or generous person. I would say yes because I felt like people were taking score, and I wanted to always be on the winning side (even though, as is general with people who perpetually say yes, I hardly ever asked anyone for anything). But the yeses nearly took me out. I realized that saying yes to everyone else, was, in essence, the equivalent to saying no to myself. No, my personal time and space isn't important. No, sleep is optional and it is reasonable to expect myself to accomplish multiple tasks in a day. No, I don't deserve a moment to breathe or a moment of reprieve. No, I'm not important - everyone else is.

When I learned to say no, I realized that it did not require an explanation, and that "no" is an adequate one word response. There didn't have to be a substantial reason why. No, I didn't need an excuse or grand reason that I didn't want to participate in an event, or a guest lecture in a class, or attend a workshop, or go to dinner, or review this book or this article, or go out on a date, or join a club or support group, or be a mentor or advisor. No.

Sometimes it (the no) is needed simply because I am tired, overwhelmed, depressed, moody, or otherwise distracted. Other times it is because my plate is already full, overflowing with the residue of other unintentional or well-meaning yeses. And sometimes, it is because I simply don't want to, don't have any interest or desire to, and would prefer to indulge in doing something else or nothing at all.

No, I don't have other plans or a laundry list of chores to accomplish first;

No, I am not sick or bedridden;

No, I don't have a deadline or a stack of papers to grade;

No, I just don't want to.

I don't feel like it.

I have a date with myself: a bubble bath, glass of wine, mellow music and all, and I'm not breaking it. I have had a long day, week, or month and I just want to chill. I need some personal, one-on-one time: just me and my reflection in the mirror time. No, no, no!

So, in the spirit of knowing how to say no… I have the following suggestions that I have learned over the years (I am in my late 30's):

1. Always say "no" first. Do not allow "yes" to be your default answer. It is easier to go back later and say yes, than it is to go back later and say no.

2. Never agree to do something on the spot. Always take some time to think about it and consider whether or not it is going to be an imposition. If it is, say no.

3. Limit yourself on how many things you agree to do (beyond your comfort zone) every month/semester/year, etc., I say "yes" to three things beyond my regular responsibilities every academic semester. After that, I almost always (depending on the request) say no. NOTE: I say beyond my regular responsibilities, which already leave me with limited personal time.

4. Never compromise your peace. If you have a full plate, acknowledge it. Don't try to overcompensate for a previous "no" with a present "yes." Never agree to do something you are not comfortable doing or that will stretch you beyond your limits. You do not owe anybody anything!

5. If you have a choice (and clearly, sometimes, whether it be for personal or professional reasons, you don't), reserve the right to decline or say no.

6. Save some "yeses" for yourself. Women have the tendency to put other people's needs and priorities above their own. Self-care is not selfish and even if it were, we deserve a bit of self-indulgence every now and then. Don't say yes to something that is essentially saying "no" to yourself. Take care of yourself.

7. Don't apologize for saying no. You have every right to decline a request or refuse an opportunity. You should not feel like you are doing something wrong, being rude, disrespectful, or obstinate. No is the alternative option to yes. It is a neutral response, neither positive nor negative (regardless of the requestor's reaction).

8. It is not a sin to change your mind. Don't feel locked into something just because you may have agreed to do it in the past. Circumstances change. Your number one obligation should be to yourself. Period. Being that this book is about empowering ourselves, here are a few things to remember as we begin to say no and set boundaries in our lives. Start by identifying your thoughts, feelings, and wants. Think of what you want to communicate and how you want to phrase your message. Be as specific and as clear as possible about what you want, think, and feel. Vague or tentative statements will likely lead to misinterpretation by the other person. Recognize, be honest with, and honor your desires and feelings.

"Own" your message. Acknowledge that your message comes from your frame of reference and your perceptions. You can acknowledge ownership with personalized "I" statements such as "I don't agree with you" (as compared to "You're wrong"). Actually use the word "no" when declining. "No" has more power and is less ambiguous than,

"Well, I just don't think so... " or "I really shouldn't..." Make sure your nonverbal gestures mirror your verbal messages. Shake your head when saying "no." Often people unknowingly nod their heads and smile when they are attempting to decline or refuse. Avoid feeling guilty. It is not up to you to solve others' problems or make them happy. Ask for feedback and then listen carefully to the other person. Asking for feedback can make it clear to the other person that you are expressing an opinion, a feeling, or a desire, rather than a demand. Listening to their feedback and engaging in a discussion can correct any misperceptions that either of you have. Encourage others to be clear, direct, and specific in their feedback to you.

In doing these things, saying no helps us make room for the important yeses in our lives - the yeses that nourish and serve us. Saying no leaves us with more time, energy and even better health. It's how we can listen to ourselves, stand up for ourselves and practice compassionate self-care.

Sometimes, saying no is tough because we're caught off guard, or feel guilty, or don't think we have the permission to decline. To ease the tension (in both ourselves and in the conversation), we blurt out "Sure! I don't mind!" But then our body twists, and we feel like we can't go back. So we do the very thing we don't want to do - we become miserable and start to feel resentment toward the other person, or ourselves.

Writing a list in advance can help. This is because it gives you the opportunity to reflect on the requests, habits, ideas, and people that you'd like to say no to. It lets you think through your priorities and values and serves as a reminder. (For instance, you can keep this list on your phone, in your wallet or in your bag.)

If you're not sure where to start, think of the times you've said "yes," and when you've regretted doing so. Think of the things that deprive you of happiness. Think of the things that uplift you, and what you might have to say no to, in order to make space for these things in your life.

When creating your list, be specific. Think of your list as a set of personal guidelines or guiding principles. After each "no" statement, you also can include *why* you're saying no. Your "why" gives you the courage - and inspiration - to decline: because you truly understand the pivotal reason why saying no is essential.

Read your list aloud. Declare your no's out loud. Practice saying no until it becomes natural to you (or as natural as you can make it for yourself).

Here's a sample list of what types of things that you might say no to:

- Requests that elicit a physical discomfort.
- Requests that don't sound like fun.
- Requests that will inevitably make you resentful.
- Requests of *any kind*.
- Magazines, shows and other forms of media that make you feel bad about yourself.
- Food that doesn't taste good.
- Workouts that don't feel good.
- Clothes that don't make you feel beautiful or the way you'd like to feel.
- Events you don't feel enthusiastic about.

- Spending time with people who drain you of energy. You might not be able to avoid these people entirely, but you can minimize your time with them.

- More than five tasks on your to-do list per day.

- Perpetuating, feeding, and fueling the negative, limiting thoughts of your inner critic.

- Channel-surfing (instead of making time for the programs you actually want to watch).

- Multitasking.

- Calorie-counting.

- Questioning your worth.

- Conversations about horrible bodies, and the calories in your pasta.

- Hyper-worrying about what others think about you.

- Rigid eating rules, such as not eating after a certain time (when you're clearly hungry).

- Stores whose ads promote narrow beauty standards or sexually objectify kids, teens, or really anyone.

- Anything in your home that feels suffocating emotionally.

- Judging yourself for experiencing negative emotions. Give yourself the permission to feel them all.

- Assumptions that you cannot do something. (I work on this every day.)

- Dismissing your likes, preferences, wants and desires. Instead, listen to your brain. Try to be open to everything.

Again, this list of no's is just an example. I just wanted to show the many, many things that we can say no to. The many areas where we have permission to say no. Some of the statements might resonate with you. Others might not. Your own list might look completely different. But whatever your list looks like, don't forget: You have all the reason in the world to say no to anything or anyone.

Reinforcing Your Boundaries

Think your boundaries might need some reinforcing? Here are some ideas to get you started:

Know yourself. The starting point in setting boundaries is with you. What do you need to have in place in your life, day to day, to feel at your best? Nobody knows you like you - your body, your emotions, and your spirit.

Get specific. What does a good day look like for you? Think about what helps you to feel your best, including your ideal activity level, the types of activities, your amount of time for rest, time with people and alone, the kinds of foods that make you feel good. And also think about what gets in the way of what could otherwise be a good day, including over-work, lack of rest, not listening to your body on days when you don't feel well, and people who bring drama and negativity. Knowing what you need to do to take care of yourself is empowering.

Set realistic standards. One of the biggest reasons for not enforcing your own boundaries is feeling like you need to be all things, to all people, all the time. That's a lot to ask of yourself. Perfectionism is a trap, leading you to say yes when you should say no, often followed by exhaustion and resentment. So look in the mirror and repeat after me: "I don't have to be perfect." Your value as a human being doesn't depend on how much you turn yourself inside out by pleasing others. Give yourself permission to treat yourself with tender loving care.

Start communicating your boundaries. Let people know what you can and can't do. You don't have to give a big speech and hope everybody takes you seriously. Instead, communicate boundaries in the moment, like when someone asks you to do something you don't want to do, or don't feel like doing, or asks you to commit to a future activity when you aren't ready to do so.

Enforce gently. Repeat as needed. Most likely, the people in your life will be taken by surprise when you start to set limits with them. Using phrases like, "Sorry, I can't do that," or, "That wouldn't be good for me," or, "I have to schedule this for later," can get the message across without being confrontational. But remember that you may need to enforce your boundaries repeatedly, over time, to be understood. You've probably heard the old saying - hope springs eternal.

Leave the guilt at the door. Whether intended or not, a no may result in a guilt trip from the person you say no to. If you encounter the "But, why? question, followed by, "But I thought… " then be prepared to have your guilt button pushed. Remember you are in control here. Don't feel like you have to make excuses for yourself or explain yourself away; don't push yourself to negotiate unless you want to.

Take time to prepare for problem situations. We all find ourselves in situations where setting limits with ourselves or with others will be especially difficult. It can help to have a strategy in place in advance. You might want to rehearse what you will say or do if temptations - or triggers - arise. Decide what situations you will avoid, and how you will react. Have a safety plan in place, including an escape plan if needed. Enlisting someone to support you can help.

Watch the blaming. It's easy to fall into the trap of blaming other people for making demands on us, or for putting temptations in front of us. But don't assume other people are automatically out there to take advantage of you or to distract you from your self-care goals. Sometimes they just don't know any better. It may be that you haven't communicated your boundaries in a way they can understand, or they need a few more gentle reminders. Let other people be who they are. Remember you can't control their expectations, but you can control how much you intend to deliver on these expectations.

It Starts with You

Lastly, remember that enforcing your boundaries begins with you. Give yourself some encouragement to stay within the limits you have set, so as to take good care of yourself physically, emotionally, and spiritually. Give yourself a pat on the back for doing the best you can, and don't criticize yourself for not being perfect.

By the way, with the holidays approaching, this is a great time to review your boundaries in advance of the season of over-expectation, over-commitment and over-indulgence.

Enforcing boundaries is a long process, conducted moment by moment, one step at a time. And remember, if you are taking good care of yourself, you will be that much better able to care for the important people in your life.

Contact Information:

Lindsay J. Hallead, MCOM, MA, CLC

Email: ljhallead@gmail.com

Phone: 231.239.1950

Facebook: Northern Michigan New Path

Chiwa Higashi

Chiwa is a Divine Messenger, Intuitive Life Coach, Energy Worker, Spiritual Teacher, Author, Speaker.

She works with Arch Angels and Masters from higher realm, and has been sharing divine messages and healing gifts to support humanity in the ascension process.

Her purpose is to empower women, so they can find their own power, help them to remember who they truly are, achieve their goals and live their dreams.

Using her intuitive gifts, clairvoyance, and Spirit communication, she helps women find their own gifts and life purposes, identify any blocks and limitations, clear them, and support them in fulfilling their life purposes.

Chiwa can access to Akashic Record, use the information and guidance to assist women to transform their lives. Her goal is to help all women to awaken to the truth, and achieve total freedom at all levels: physical, financial, emotional, spiritual, and soul.

She also has a mission to support highly sensitive children, who are evolved souls, help them remember who they are, and accomplish their mission on Earth.

Chiwa knows that everyone is divine pure love and light, and she is here to assist humanity actualize Heaven on Earth.

My Journey Into The Heart

By Chiwa Higashi

I was born and grew up on a tiny island called Koshiki-island in Japan. I was always surrounded by nature, ocean, and mountains. Whenever I am in nature, I feel that I am home.

People in my village were very kind, giving, and caring. That was the way for everyone. Whenever my Mom cooked some yummy food, it was my job to deliver some of it to neighbors, so they could have some, too. Sharing, and helping each other were natural ways for people to express love. I grew up knowing that the world was a safe place to be and people were naturally good. I still believe it is true.

I had a good family - my parents and three brothers. I was the second born, and only girl, so I was treated differently than my brothers. My parents were typical Japanese parents. Dad worked and earned money to support our family. And my Mom cooked, cleaned, and took care of the children. Even though we didn't have much money or material things, we were blessed and we always had enough to share with others.

The people on the island lived the way it had always been, never questioning changes, probably from generation to generation. Harmony in the community was very important, so most people seldom expressed their true feelings nor ideas. My Mom accepted their way and followed others as a woman, even though she didn't agree. My Dad was different. He had visions and he wanted to change people's lives, and he eventually did.

As a family we had fun and we laughed. However, I saw and experienced some painful situations. My parents were struggling financially and they were stressed out. My Dad was a very loving soul, but sometimes when he got drunk, he expressed his emotions verbally toward my mom. As a sensitive child, I felt what was going on and it affected my path without even knowing it.

We were supposed to fit and keep harmony in the community, but I didn't fit at all. I was different. I didn't want to follow rules and be told what to do. I sometimes gave my Mom hard time. Deep inside I was lonely and feeling that nobody understood me or knew who I really was.

I always had a desire for freedom. I wanted to be free from my home and everything, even though I loved my family and my island. I used to stand on a beach looking at the horizon, wondering what was out there in the world.

One day I saw a vision of high rise buildings. It was just like New York, even though I didn't see a Statue of Liberty, a symbol of freedom.

After I graduated from middle school, I left the island and moved to a city on the Main land to attend high school. While I was in high school, my Dad ran election to become a Mayor and I helped him with the campaign. I went with him town to town, making speeches, greeting people, and asking them to vote for him. At first I was scared to speak in public, but I got used to it. People often shed tears when they heard my speech and I hoped that I had helped my Dad get some votes. In spite of all our efforts, he lost the election and it was a big disappointment for all of us. Financially, it was devastating for my family, but my Dad found a way to move forward, and four years later he won and became a Mayor. After years of hard work, he changed people's lives on the island, and made all his dreams come true. As a result he received a medal of honor from the Emperor of Japan for his contribution. Of course this medal belonged to my Mom also, without her support, he couldn't have accomplished anything.

I learned that if I never gave up my dreams and kept moving forward, all would become true. Even today, Spirit within me is always giving me the power and courage to keep on going until I realize all my dreams..

After I graduated from high school I got a job, hoping to help my family financially. I moved to my uncle's house in Osaka and started to work for an oil company. As a free spirit, I felt like I was in a box. I wanted to do something more fun.

One day, I came up with this great idea of playing in a theater and creating fun shows to make people laugh. I saw a program on TV and I went for an audition to join this company. Luckily, I was accepted! I was very excited about my new career. I told my parents about it, but my Dad disagreed and even told me that he would no longer consider me as his daughter. I was very disappointed. I didn't know what else to do but to give it up. After that, my life started to fall apart. I needed a change.

I decided to do something totally different and chose to come to America to study English. Honestly, I just wanted to get away from everything and be free. My parents didn't like the idea and they wanted me to stay. However, I had already made up my mind, and they had to accept. I gave them a hard time, but I had to follow what my heart was guiding me to do. It was my first step toward freedom.

I arrived in Los Angeles with excitement. It was my first time in America. Everything was new and different for me. I stayed with a host family, a single Mom with three boys, and my job was to help her with cooking, cleaning, laundry, and taking care of the boys, in exchange for room and board. She gave me $10 a week for allowance. I still wanted freedom - left the host family and got an apartment with a friend. At night, I worked at a Japanese restaurant as a waitress for minimum wage, and continued my schooling during the day. I was enjoying freedom my own way.

Life went on, I got married and had two beautiful children. Having children changed my life forever. As a Mom, I experienced true love through my children. I felt fulfilled as I gave them all my love and care.

During that time, I was guided to learn meditation, and started to get into spirituality and healing. I took clairvoyant training, and also learned different modalities of healing. As I did more healing on myself, I became more aware of my inner self and my life. The energy I didn't know existed started to surface. It was a beginning of my awakening.

In this process, all of my negative emotions and feelings started to come up. I knew that my relationship with my husband wasn't going well. I was frustrated and angry deep inside. I was taking care of the children, cooking, cleaning, and doing most of the chores. I felt like that I wasn't getting any support, especially emotionally. (This was my view at that time. In truth, he was supporting me).

I started to question my existence. I felt like I was a bird in a cage who wanted to fly freely but couldn't. I was dying deep inside. It was my soul's calling to wake up. I thought I wouldn't live very long, so I wrote a book for my children to share what I wanted to tell them. I realized that I didn't have much sense of who I really was. It was a painful time for all of us.

One day, like a flash of light, a knowing came to me that I had a choice: I could continue living the same way I always did, or choose something new and different. I realized that I could change my life by choosing something new. Out of love for my children, I wanted to keep on going and live. That moment shifted my consciousness and changed my life forever. This knowing and power was truly a gift from the Divine.

I decided to start my life all over again and chose to get a divorce. It wasn't easy for all of us, but I believed it was the best choice. It was our soul agreement to go through this to bring healing to all of us.

After the divorce, I moved to the mountains. I meditated, prayed, walked in the forest, and wrote messages to share with people. Quietness and peace in the mountains helped my heart to heal.

Even though I was doing some healing work to help people, I wasn't making enough money to cover everything. I had to do something else to increase my income.

I always had a strong desire for success and financial freedom. It was deep inside me and it was like my soul's mission. I had a dream to help my children, family, people, especially women, to be free at all levels. I had big dreams. To actualize my dreams, I had to be wealthy enough to give freely.

My entrepreneur spirit awakened deep inside me and I started my first home based business without knowing anything about business or the real world. I failed time and time again, but I kept on going. I didn't give up. I went to many seminars, events, and talks to learn from successful leaders, and also spiritually awakened teachers. My vision was strong enough to keep me going.

During that time, I experienced struggle, pain, and disappointment. My path to awakening wasn't an easy one. At one point, I lost almost everything and felt like I didn't have anything left. All I had was unwavering faith in God, and I knew, somehow, that everything would be ok. While I was learning to succeed in business, I continued healing work and teaching. But I started to feel people's pain (also my own), and it became too much for me. I decided to let go of everything and get away from the world.

I went into the mountains and spent most of my time meditating and praying. I was tested many times to give my ego-self up and surrender all to God. Every time when I didn't know what to do, but totally surrendered everything to God, somehow miracles happened. What kept me safe and alive is truly a gift from God. The love and power from God within me worked miracles, and I always came out into the Light. God provided everything I needed at each moment and I am so grateful.

The path to success is a process of becoming who you are meant to be. It is an awakening process to remember who you are and your life purpose. I am grateful that I have learned from amazing people in business and spirituality fields. I continue to learn, grow, and evolve as a soul, and I am grateful that I can support others in their awakening process.

There are no coincidences in life. If you are reading this message, you are born to bring change into the world. You may not fit in your family or society. You may have felt alone or you may have felt that nobody understood you. Please know that you are perfect just the way you are. You are an awakened soul. It is time for you to celebrate your uniqueness and be yourself. There is nothing wrong with you.

Just like me, you may have been born to clear ancestral patterns, to bring a new way of living to free yourself, your family, and humanity. As you clear all that doesn't serve you any longer, you are helping everyone also. We are connected as One. Your choices affect all humanity. When you awaken, you help others awaken.

You may be experiencing challenges in your life right now. Please know that you are always supported and loved unconditionally. I can assure you that everything will work out perfectly, if you surrender and allow the Universe to help you. Take a deep breath, relax, and let go.

You are here with purpose. Your presence on Earth is very important. You are playing a role in the world that no one else can. Without you, the world is not complete. You have a God given gift within you. It is your job to find what it is and use it to help others. Then your purpose will be fulfilled. Go deep within your heart and find out.

You are not a victim. You are not your story nor your past. Have the courage to break free from illusions of lack and limitation. When you focus on here and now fully, you are free. There is no past nor future. Now is all you have. Life is a continuation of this now moment.

You are not your body or mind. You exist beyond this physical world and you are infinite. You are pure awareness. You are infinite possibilities and you can choose to create anything you desire. You are the creator of your reality.

Awakening is happening in all of us and Mother Earth. Old ways are falling away. New ways are emerging. You are here to lead others to the New Way, which is based on Love, and Oneness for all humanity. It all starts within you.

In order for you to change your life and your reality, you must choose something new. Also you have to change the vibration within you.

Everything is energy. Your thoughts, feelings, and beliefs are also energy. How you vibrate inside will reflect into the outer world as your experience. When you raise your vibration, you raise your consciousness.

How can we shift our vibration?

Your awareness is the first step. Become aware of what is happening within you and around. Don't resist, just allow and accept as is. When you fully accept what is, you have the power to change it.

Allow old emotions to come up and be released. When you allow yourself to feel whatever is inside, it will leave your body. Have courage to go through this process and be free.

Do something you really love. Focus on things that will bring feelings of joy. Sing, dance, laugh, and listen to the music that will uplift you.

Go into nature and connect with divine energy. Mountains, trees, flowers, ocean, will help you raise your vibration. Connect with Mother Earth and ground yourself. She will support you.

Forgive yourself and others. Forgiveness is the key to peace and freedom. Truly, there is nothing to forgive. Because at the soul level, everything was planned before you were even born. Your soul chose that experience for your soul evolution.

Be grateful for all you have and all that you are. Feeling of gratitude always opens your heart and helps you come back to love.

Let go of your mind, and go into the heart and listen. Listen in silence. You will know what your soul is communicating with you. All you have been seeking is in your heart. Please remember to create your reality from your heart, not from your mind. If you create in your mind, you create a world of duality. When you create in your heart, you create a world of oneness and love. Remember to live in your heart.

If you need some healing support, ask for professional help. An Energy clearing session will help you shift your vibration. You don't have to do it all by yourself. There are many energy workers and they are willing to support you in your ascension process (I am one of them). Ask God and Angels for support. It is given instantly.

It is not easy to walk on Earth with full awareness as a master. Please know that you are already a master. It is time for you to remember.

The world needs Your Light right now. Let Your Light Shine.

Together we can create Heaven on Earth.

Never ever give up on your dreams. I believe in you. You can do it.

Spread your wings and fly!

I would like to complete my story with a happy ending…

I studied theater in college and I had so much fun! One of my dreams came true. My dad spent the last part of his life writing and creating arts and he was very loving and peaceful. He is now very happy and free in heaven.

My Mom is in a great shape, and at age 90, she still rides a bicycle all over town. She keeps saying, "I am so happy and blessed," because she doesn't have to cook for others unless she chooses to, or take care of anyone. She is now free to do anything she wants. Both of my children are now grown, and courageously following their path to live their dreams. I feel so blessed to have them in my life!

My life continues to unfold as the Divine directs me at each moment. I am on my way to live all my dreams and help others to do the same. I learned that there was nothing to fear. When you follow your heart, somehow everything will work out perfectly. My journey into the heart was the journey to the Love of All That was. All is well.

And my story continues to the next chapter of my life.

In closing, from the bottom of my heart, I would like to thank Jim & Jim for this wonderful opportunity to share my message. Thank you, Jim and Jim. I also thank my parents Kazuchika and Toshiko Higashi, my family, my mother-in-law Marian McAllister, my children Madoka and Takumi McAllister, and all those who loved and supported me over the years. Without them, I am not here as I am.

I thank God and the Angels for guiding, directing, and helping me every moment,

and YOU, who is reading this message, for being here on Earth. I honor your courage in remembering who you truly are, and live your dreams.

Keep Your Light Shine!

I love you. You are amazing!

Chiwa's contact information:

Chiwa Higashi

P O Box 4444, Boulder

Colorado 80306-4444, USA

303-215-6073

ShineLightNow@gmail.com

Skype: chiwa.higashi

http://www.ShineLightNow.com/english

http://www.TeensAwake.com

Mavis Mazhura, MA

Mavis Mazhura is an author, public speaker and corporate trainer for the past six years. She is an authorized and official certified SDI facilitator of Personal Strength South Africa in applying Relationship awareness in life, certified Emotional Intelligence, Critical Conversations, Personal Energy Management, Creativity and Innovation Trainer. She is also a certified John Maxwell Leadership Trainer and Coach. Her passion is equipping and empowering individuals to expand human awareness and reach their full potential. She has one on one and group coaching programs. Mavis has trained from lower to board level management teams in Uganda, Botswana, South Africa, Zimbabwe and Namibia. Mavis specializes in Human Behavior and Human Factor Programs. She is the author of *Navigating the Rapids and the Waves of Life: Managing Emotions for Success: 10 Lessons for Managing Emotions for Success*. Mavis Mazhura is a Human Behavior Specialist and the cofounder of Training B2B CC, a training company based in Johannesburg, South Africa.

From Awareness to Transformation

By Mavis Mazhura, MA

"It may be hard for an egg to turn into a bird: it would be a jolly sight harder for it to learn to fly while remaining an egg. We are like eggs at present. And you cannot go on indefinitely being just an ordinary, decent egg. We must be hatched or go bad."

- C.S. Lewis

From awareness to transformation is a journey of personal change. Any small and seemingly insignificant changes in our day-to-day lives - to the big and almost incomprehensible changes in world history - begin at the individual level. For us to improve our lives, and society as a whole, we ought to be challenging the individual's *status quo*, continually. If we do not change, nothing in our lives improves - not even the things around us.

Nelson Mandela once said: *"There is nothing like returning to a place that remains unchanged to find the ways in which you yourself have altered."* Personal change is about altering ourselves – but also removing any conditioning to return to our default state of being. As we are born into this world and start growing, we begin to conform to the influences around us, and these influences that shape us, normally distort who we really are at the core.

These distortions take peace away from us - causing pain and strain as our hearts continually yearn for us to be more, to do more, and to fulfill our reason for being here. This pain and strain in many instances pushes us to change for the better or for the worse - based on the different levels of awareness. We either change by adding more distortions or creating distractions that take us further from who we truly are, or we remove the distortions. When one removes distortions there is positive change, and the pain and strain begins to disappear, and any other challenges coming your way, you can handle with grace.

This differentiates a few from the masses that decide to live with distortions - either intentionally or unintentionally. So, if we want to change things, we have to not only understand them, but to change ourselves first. Changing self leads to a change in perception, a shift in beliefs, and transformation of one's identity. Change is about motion or movement, and any movement requires energy.

Changing ourselves means shifting our energy levels. Like the egg hatching, change is the process of opening the shell of distortions that enclose our understanding, so that we can return to what Panache Desai – a contemporary thought leader and author of *Discovering Your Soul Signature* – calls our soul signature, our purpose, or our default state of being. We realize that we have to return to our original form, to our purpose - like the egg came from a chicken, it has to be a chicken again. Change requires energy or transforming energy to change its form.

We are living in times of high energy demand, because of rapid changes and increased complexity. These times also require that we transform energy faster, as the turbulence of rapid change is constantly throwing us off balance - hence the constant misalignment. We find ourselves with less and less time, everything becoming more complicated, and people becoming more unfaithful, demanding more from their lives, and becoming intoxicated with negative energy. Our energy levels expand either positively or negatively, and amplify or diminish our experience or relationship with our surroundings - which include money, family, health, spiritual, mental and social issues, and our careers. Many are going through emotional roller coasters or are simply stuck with negative emotions. Our EMOTIONS are ENERGY. They fuel us to take action or incapacitate us to inaction.

Energy is the fuel that makes change happen and what makes us accomplish our goals in life. This depends on whether you want to accomplish something destructive or constructive. You need energy to start moving from where you are - to where you want to be. At any given point in our lives we have energy - either positive or negative, low or high - activating us or deactivating us. However, I would assume that we all want to do good, to love and to be loved, which is the true essence of humanity, and when we are being that we are operating at our highest energy frequency. However, sometimes we fail, we falter, we get distracted or move away from our default state of being - which is love. This is due to focusing on external distortions, a loss of perspective, or the inability to respond to what is happening around us - from our inner being where energy can easily be transformed. Energy in human beings includes emotional energy, mental energy, and physical energy.

Research has proven that emotional energy is more powerful because it can incapacitate the mental and physical energy. Any alteration or transformation we make at the emotional level can change the mental and physical energy. To achieve optimal performance or attain flow, these three energies need to be integrated. You have to think what you feel and act out your thoughts - and have feelings in synchronicity with the awareness of the thoughts and feelings - and the outcomes that we want to accomplish. One of the laws of the universe is the law of vibration. This law is about how energy levels change, how we have the ability to transform energy, and how energy changes form. Any change we experience - whether intentional or unintentional - means a change in the scale of energy to either a low or high vibration. However, when we are aware, and have willingness and the discipline to transform and direct our energy constantly towards the goals we want, then - POSITIVE CHANGE is inevitable.

Why change?

I think there is only one reason we change:

To return to our default state of being - which is LOVE, to enhance FLOW.

We are created to flow, given that 65% of our bodies are water. However, sometimes distortions cause us to solidify or stagnate, and this causes us to be unfulfilled. We then change because we see that change is the only way to gain fulfillment, and we gain fulfillment by loving. We have to keep transforming in order to create a new world for ourselves and others, to renew our perception of the old, to empower the present experience, or to avoid pain in the future. We change because we have a thorn in the flesh. This is an indication of the misalignment of the internal world with our external world. This causes pain - and the only way is to change and return to love is to enhance flow. When you're not achieving success or the results you want in any relationship - with money, family (parents, spouse, children and siblings), your body (thoughts, emotions and physical), job, spiritual life, friends and lifestyle - you yearn to change or are forced to change or shift your energy levels to your default state.

But change isn't easy...

"After living with their dysfunctional behavior for so many years (a sunk cost if ever there was one), people become invested in defending their dysfunctions rather than changing them." - Marshall Goldsmith

You would assume that change is as easy as the many times you hear about it. Everyone knows change has to happen, but in reality many people get stuck in the process of change. They get stuck with the results they do not want, whether it is a relationship, financial status, a job, a physical outlook, or a lifestyle. And this is not because they do not have good thoughts about what good needs to be done for them to get the results they want. They have all the good thoughts, but there is no movement from where they are to where they want to be.

Sometimes we all know what has to be done for change to happen - but we keep repeating the dysfunctional behaviors. So, while thoughts are good, if you do not feel your thoughts - that is give your thoughts energy in the direction you want - you are simply not going anywhere. Many people are not integrated; they have positive thoughts and negative emotions and the result is to be STUCK! To change we have to transform our emotions - our internal energy - for motion to take place. With change starting at the individual level, this is also where the friction occurs, and inertia and decision paralysis keep people stuck in their old ways. Chip Heath and Dan Heath, authors of *SWITCH, How to change things when change is hard* indicated that the change process is: SEE-FEEL-CHANGE.

SEE-ING is about creating or having self-awareness, and knowing your values, traits, self image and motives. These values, traits, self image and motives are your identity, the foundation of your behavior patterns, and your emotional triggers. One also has to see the foundation of your identity, and the models that shaped it. Your values are what you feel are important, self image is how you feel about yourself, traits are your choice of behavior based on how it makes you feel, and your motives are why you feel. Seeing and knowing are not enough. Like as I said before, most people know what they need to do in order to change - but they still do not do it. Many people are also stuck defending an identity which is causing them pain due to a lack of fulfillment. This is largely because of lack of integration between the mental energy (thoughts-awareness), emotional energy (emotions-feel) and physical energy (action-change). After seeing or having awareness, we need to identify if what we are feeling inside us is in alignment with our thoughts. When thoughts and feelings are in alignment, action or change is automatic, but when they are not aligned, 99% of the time the emotional energy WINS. For positive change to happen, we have to constantly stretch our identity. The self-awareness that develops from seeing yourself clearly in a non-judgmental way, may involve asking the right questions, seeing the source of your character, behavior patterns, beliefs, traits, self image, motives and values.

We are not born with an identity (beliefs, self image, traits and values). We are born with one motive - which is to love and to receive love. Any motive we have outside of love is a distortion of who we truly are and it causes us pain. Any element of our identity that distorts love, will lead to a lack of fulfillment. In pursuit of who we are, we have sought things like significance, variety, certainty, contribution and growth. If we love enough, these things happen automatically; we become significant, we begin to contribute, we grow, we create certainty, and we can handle uncertainty. In developing awareness we have to be willing to see how we have distorted who we are, the foundation of our identity, the way we perceived it, and ask if it enhanced or distorted who we are. Most distortions occur from birth up to the age of 15 years, and sometimes in adult life due to negative experiences, and sometimes from positive experiences as well.

However, distortions that occur from birth up to 15 years of age require much effort to change or even to be able to see them. This is because at this age individuals are unable to rationalize the events or influences they mostly feel. The feelings may be enhancing who we are or distorting things, causing us to move away from love and flow. Many live with these distortions without seeing them, or simply settle for mediocrity. These distortions sabotage these people's fulfillment and others may decide to live a life dominated by negativity. However, others - due to the continual discomfort caused by these distortions - are forced to seek change.

Examples of distortions which occur as we grow up may be an insecure parent who could be aggressive with one child - who may, as a result, grow up with insecurity or become aggressive as well. So, the parent had distortions which they projected onto the child. Another example of a distortion is that one child is favored and given special status by the parent, and this child grows up feeling special and with a sense of being entitled: expecting everyone to make them feel special. Another child may have grown up in an abusive home and they can either become independent or controlling. This is a distortion away from who they really are - which is LOVE. Love has no connotation of 'I am more special,' or barriers.

Any negative emotion experienced due to any distortion creates barriers, and the barriers are sabotaging our essence. When we create barriers due to negative emotions, we engage in behaviors that cement these distortions into our brain and behavior patterns – if we do not discard them. Seeing also involves acknowledging trapped emotions due to distortions from the past - so as to find ways to discard them. This way CHANGE happens. It is also about a reality check. Where am I and where do I need to go, and why are results the way they are right now? It is seeing things the way the are now, and the gap between where you are and where you want to be.

FEEL-ING the emotion - whether positive or negative - is the process of change. Denied, suppressed and repressed emotions are traps for change, and they will trip you up backwards. It is difficult, if not impossible, to process any emotion you cannot identify, acknowledge, and experience. Many people try to escape negative emotions by projecting them outwards, enduring them, or covering up what they truly feel. Both positive and negative emotions are useful tools for change - but only if you intentionally use them for change.

For example, disgust with oneself can make you change if you don't run away from the emotion and use a temporary anesthetic to dampen the feeling like smoking, alcohol and sex. Resolve can make one change, and interest can make one change. Gary Craig, founder of the Emotional Freedom Technique, indicated that addictions are born out of people who fail to transform negative emotions.

Going through change is about constantly navigating and transforming negative emotions, challenging the status quo, patterns, and beliefs that may have been successful in the past, and experimenting with different ways of 'feeling' due to the different options that could be considered for going forward. The longer you experience the emotion, the more one begins to normalize it.

Changing might mean letting go of that normalized, known state of being. And for many, this causes discomfort due to anxiety, worry and the fear it causes because of letting go of the known. Feeling must be connected to seeing, and not separated from it, because if you see without feeling, change will not happen - and if you feel without seeing, change will not happen. As you feel your emotions, see their source or triggers - so you can transform them. Remember that our identity triggers all our emotions, and for change to occur, our identity has to be constantly stretched. Also bear in mind that your identity is the sum total of your past experiences, and if you do not consciously revisit it, it may be distorted due to past experiences perceived as being negative. Your identity may also be tied up with a lot of negative emotions.

Anthony Robbins, the life success coach, said that you can not achieve a goal that is bigger than your identity. Any effort towards change that violates one's identity will fail. One has to question and understand the dominant emotions as a result of your identity. For example, how do you feel about your key values when you are living them out, or when you are not getting support? When did this feeling start? What was happening? How do you feel about yourself; is your self image positive or negative in all your relationships (with money, people, your body, spirituality and career)? How do you feel about your traits - both positive and negative? What unmet needs do you have that are strengthening your identity? What are your dominant emotions that relate to your identity? Are they enhancing your default state of being, which is LOVE?

Could you be holding on to an identity which is causing you pain, and are you also afraid of changing it? To lessen the power of the fear of change, which keeps many people stuck, one should start imagining how you would feel if you achieved your goals or fulfilled your unmet needs. One has to hold on to that feeling long enough, until movement begins to happen. If there is resistance, a release of past negative emotions has to happen. We are not victims of our emotions - we can release or transform them. Emotions are the lubricants that make movement from 'seeing' to 'doing' occur. And here transformation begins to happen - and if we can feel it, we can do it.

CHANG-ING is about bringing the seeing and the feeling into alignment – and that is self-transformation.

"The most important journey you will take in your life will usually be the one of self transformation. Often, this is the scariest because it requires the greatest changes, in your life." - Shannon L. Alder

Our personal victories come as a result of our transformation. Self-awareness is the foundation of transformation. Transformation is about expanding one's identity (values, self image, traits and motives), and our inner world that triggers emotions to either get things done or not to get them done. In expanding our inner world, we have to release the negative emotions and to let go of patterns, beliefs and neuro-associations that do not serve us.

Dr. Demartini, a human behavior specialist, indicated that our values form as a result of our voids - what we perceive as missing. These perceived voids are our unmet needs which we seek to fulfill in life, or it forces us to return to our default. All that is missing for us to be fulfilled is LOVE. However, in identity formation, one may form values, self image, and traits that are a defense mechanism - in an effort to protect oneself from the pain resulting from unmet needs. This identity that is formed in our early years in life needs to be revisited in adult life to allow one to choose an identity that is aligned, or congruent with one's mission, vision or purpose.

Change can be overwhelming. It is important to compartmentalize it so that it is manageable. So, once you realize your identity needs to be stretched, you can look at one aspect at a time - for example your values - and work on them in order to align them with where your heart wants to take you. The reason for change is to love and to feel loved. When you do what you love, love is all around and success follows, and when you love yourself, you can love others and others can love you. In order to change, assess the key areas of your life (career, spiritual, mind and body, finances, family and social) and ask yourself - where is LOVE missing? Which area - if I created love - would have a ripple effect in other areas? Your purpose will make you love without trying and love becomes automatic. Change becomes an interesting journey of exploration. This way one starts conditioning oneself anew - and we FLUSH out all the distortions.

Remember we all deserve LOVE - no matter the level of our distortions, so we can find our way back to LOVE through transformation.

Contact Mavis:

Training B2B CC

Tel: +27 11 326 2499

Website: www.tb2b.co.za

Email: mavism@tb2b.co.za

Blog:www.emotions4sucess.com

Misty Anderson

Misty Anderson's natural enthusiasm and incredible heart is well suited to coaching. Her spirit, while infectious and inspiring to her clients and colleagues, is balanced by her desire to see people through not only their victories, but also the roughest patches of their lives. Her mission as a coach is to empower people to live extraordinary lives and reach their dreams with joy and intention. She is passionate about entrepreneurship, personal growth and living life to the fullest. That's quite a tall order, but Misty delights in the challenge.

Misty has consistently demonstrated the ability in her own life to set and achieve her most ambitious goals. Now she brings this experience to her coaching career with a style that is a balanced blend of support and accountability. If you seek more of what life has to offer, Misty is the coach that will get you there.

Pre-destiny or Choice

By Misty Anderson

I've heard it said that our lives are pre-destined, that we have no control over the direction and outcome of our lives.

The issue of pre-destiny is a very complicated one, which has been debated through the ages by philosophers and religious leaders alike. In almost every religion there is some reference to the nature of pre-destiny.

There are those with the commonly held belief that one's destiny is predetermination by a higher power. They claim that man has no control over anything. Everything is predetermined. As such, all that happens is the unfolding of some grand plan of destiny, known only to that higher power.

This philosophy could be very problematic when you think about it. It could lead to the question of crime and punishment, penalty and reward. If a person has no choice, then there should be neither punishment nor reward for his or her action. If a person has not choice as to the outcome he/she experiences, why do anything at all.

Just like most, I have experienced times when I felt that I had no choice, that everything was unfolding and I was not in control.

I was raised in a two parent family. Both my parents didn't graduate from high school. They had no college and no career. I found myself following in their footsteps as if I was pre-destined to be like them.

I had dreams of a better life like most people, but deep inside I thought they were just dreams that would never come true. I thought, "Who am I to have more than my parents?" "Who am I to get ahead in life?" "Who am I to have a successful career?"

Most people equate choice with freedom. It seemed so reasonable to me. Freedom means you are free to choose, right? It means you are free from restrictions. If you can't choose, then you are not free. And it would seem to follow that the more choices you have, the more freedom you have. But what I discovered is that it doesn't work out that way.

I thought, maybe if I went to college I could change my destiny. I was born in Oklahoma and made a decision to move to Chattanooga, Tennessee, live with my grandparents, and attend University of Tennessee College and get a degree. I wanted to be a lawyer because I loved debate. But like most college students, I wasn't really sure at that time what I wanted to be when I graduated.

My childhood wasn't easy. When I was very young I developed a compassion for the "underdog." I wanted to do a lot with the homeless and I wanted to make a difference in people's lives who were like me… who didn't have the skills or know what they are supposed to do based on how they were raised.

I thought when you go to college you are supposed to pick what you are going to do for the rest of your life. But when you don't have the skills to choose and your parents didn't have the skills to guide you, I felt kind of, well, just lost. I knew I was meant for something bigger I just didn't know what it was or how to get there.

I worked as a server at a local restaurant earning very good tips while working my way through college. I eventually graduated with a major in psychology and a minor in criminal justice. I thought employers would be coming out of the woodwork to give me a high-paying job. After all I am now a college graduate.

Nobody could prepare me for what happened next. After graduation in 1998 I applied for a job at Cumberland Psychiatric Hospital and they offered me a full time job at a whopping $15,000 a year. I thought, my student loans were more than that. I earned more than that in tips at the restaurant and bar tending.

A friend of mine told me if I wanted to earn more money that I needed to go into sales, so I applied and landed a job with Enterprise Rent-a-Car for $25,000 a year. I learned everything I could about selling and running a business. I went to the top in sales and eventually to manager before I was laid off in 2000.

When I found out I was pregnant and was going to be raising a child on my own, I wanted, needed, to get to that six figure income - and fast. I couldn't see that happening where I was so I decided to step out on a limb, take a chance and become a straight commission Medicare insurance agent.

For the next nine years, I worked with several Medicare providers selling Medicare insurance to seniors. I loved my job because I loved helping people. I always measured how much good I was doing for others by the amount of income I was earning.

I loved my job and I loved helping people do what's right for them. I became known a "Medicare Misty." The seniors loved me and I loved working with them. For me it was like having a thousand grandparents. It was never about what made me the next dollar. I have walked away from a sale, or given a sale away, and it always works out. I learned early on if you do the right thing, good things will always come back to you.

Everyone has a story of what they've learned along the way. This is my chance to tell mine. These are some of the things I've learned. I hope you gain some insights into your own life from what I've learned.

Believe in yourself

The opposite of "believe in yourself" is "self-doubt." When you doubt yourself, you give your power away to doubt. We've all heard those voices in our head saying, "You're not good enough." "You are going to fail." You know the voice I'm talking about. That silent whisper that haunts you when you set a goal to have and become more, and you are not sure how to get there. That voice of self-criticism when you hit a stumbling block. When you hear those voices, realize that they are not you. Those voices are past programming, past experiences, trying to keep you where you are, safe a secure.

I have found that the more you fight self-doubt the more it fights back. So here's what I do. When faced with self-doubt, STOP for a moment and ask yourself if this is really true? Ask yourself "If I proceed with this self-doubt, will it help me to accomplish my goal?" Remember, self-doubt is fear based. It's a made up story about some future event that has not, and most likely will not happen. It's not real. Let it go and move on.

I have found that just recognizing that you are experiencing self-doubt and backing away for a moment and seeing it for what it is, will weaken the self-doubt. And the more you practice it the more courageous and determined you become.

Follow your passion

We've been told what to do all our lives by our parents, teachers, professors, religious leaders and employers. When I started deciding for myself what was best for me, my life changed dramatically.

There will always be the critics out there trying to pull you down and crush your dreams. Don't listen. That's their internal dialog, not yours. That's their issues, not yours.

Make your choices and don't be afraid of what others will say. When fear grabs you, see it as a made up story that is not real. Say "Thanks for sharing but that's not me."

Remember, fear or any other negative emotion is not hanging on to you, but rather you are hanging on to it. It's your choice to hang on or let it go. I had self-doubt and plenty of it. But one day I decided if I wanted more of what life had to offer, I had to believe in myself. I had to face my self-doubt, my fears and be willing to take care of it through making the right choice.

Look at it this way. Self-doubt is a part of you that's crying for help. It needs understanding. If you want to get rid of self-doubt you have to make the right choices instead of fighting against your doubt. When you make the right choices, doubt will disappear.

Instead of doubting your abilities and asking yourself "Why? Why am I experiencing this painful situation," ask yourself instead, "What can I do to become better?" Both are a choice.

Break the cycle

The problem is that people most often go with the obvious. We rely on the same thinking, habits, behaviors and methods that we've used in the past. Go to school, get a degree, get a job, work 40 years and then retire on half of what you couldn't live on while working. That is a broken model. It doesn't work anymore. It's over. This is a 1950's model!

Look around you. There are more people choosing entrepreneurship today than ever before. If you prefer a job, that's okay, but at the same time - you'd better start thinking like an entrepreneur, because that job could be gone tomorrow.

Most people are like a fly on the window, trying harder and harder to break through, doing more of the same and getting nowhere fast. We resist new approaches because they make us feel more at risk... more uncomfortable.

But if you want rich rewards, rapidly, you must vigorously search out and implement new attitudes and behaviors. You must be willing to break free of old routines to find a better approach. You have to re-invent yourself as times change. You have to be willing to step out of your comfort zone and do something different.

What I'm saying is that your most dependable behaviors, like working the old model, can become your greatest obstacles for future success if you are not careful. They will become personal boundary lines that limit what you accomplish.

Reflect? Do you have all the time freedom you want at this point in your life? Do you take the vacations you want every year, or spend quality time with your family? Is your level of financial freedom today where you thought you would be 5 years ago? I would urge you to take a realistic look. Are you truly making progress? Are your last 5 years what you wanted? More importantly, what's your plan for the future?

I have found that there are no guarantees in life. But I do know this: for things to change in your life, *you've* got to make a change. If you want a different result you have to do something different.

The Change 2

To change you have to make two important decisions. First, you have to make a decision about the direction and vision of how you want your life to turn out. And second, you have to decide what avenue, or opportunity, you will use to take you where you want to go.

Some wait for better breaks, lower taxes, pay raises, better timing, better chances, and better opportunities. Some still continue to think that their education, the government, or "something" will eventually to save them. They think the "someday" things will get better. But what I have found is that "someday" never becomes "today" unless you make the choices to change how and what you do.

There are tremendous shifts taking place in the world today. Shifts that make it essential for low, average, and even high income earners to look at new ways by which they can supplement their earnings in order to feel secure about their future.

Today, millions are discovering that the only way out of the trap is by taking responsibility for their *own* future instead of leaving it to someone else, or to chance.

Because so few people succeed with the age-old model of, "go to school, get a job and retire in forty years," millions are turning to entrepreneurship.

I'm an entrepreneur. I own two businesses and I wouldn't think of ever doing anything different. In my coaching practice I'll show you how to step out of your comfort zone and do something different, to follow your passion, and to do it *your* way.

I have discovered that real success is about helping someone else achieve their success, so that they can help someone else. That's my mission in life.

Invest in yourself

Whatever you have in your life at this very moment is a result of how you see yourself. For example, if a person is earning a six-figure income, that's how they see themselves. And if they want to go to a higher six-figure or even a seven-figure income, they must become somebody different. The question becomes, "What do you plan to change about yourself to go from where you are now to where you want to be?

There is always something we need to change.

Maybe it's simply having a new opportunity available.

Maybe it's a matter of being fully committed to something.

Maybe it's refining your people skills or selling skills.

Maybe it's gaining greater self-confidence.

Maybe it's having the courage to take a risk.

Maybe it's overcoming self-doubt.

Our income will rarely exceed our own personal beliefs. If it does, on some rare occasion, it will quickly come back to where it was in a short period of time, that is, if we don't make a change. This is why it is critical to invest in yourself, otherwise you'll continue to produce the same results you've always produced.

Hire a coach, read uplifting and informative books, listen to personal development audios, attend seminars, etc. Learning, growing and making better choices have been the catalyst for me. My philosophy is that if I want to accomplish something but I don't know how, I find someone that is doing what I want to do and ask them for help. If it requires paying them for their knowledge, I gladly pay. Investing in yourself is the best investment you could possibly make.

When something goes wrong with your automobile, you take it to the repair shop, right? When your home air conditioner breaks down in the middle of the summer, you quickly have it repaired. When you have a serious illness that distresses your body, you go to doctor to find out what's wrong. Top performers have agents and mentors. Athletes have coaches. Where do you go when you need a check up on your own performance?

Just like a 3,000 mile check-up on your automobile or an annual visit to the doctor for a physical, you should periodically conduct your own performance self-evaluation. Ask yourself, "How am I really doing? Am I doing all I can? Am I making full use of my talents? Am I working on myself and developing the skills to go to the next level of performance? Am I just "cruising" along and maintaining "status quo" while blaming others or outside circumstances for my lack of performance? Am I living up to my full potential?" And you should answer these questions and others as objectively as possible.

And if you don't pass your check-up, seek help immediately. Hire a coach, find a mentor.

Status Quo

This may come as a shock to you, but I have found that most people really don't want to change. They would much rather to just maintain the status quo. They find that it's just easier to accept their destiny and stay on the path that's been laid for them. They spend the majority of their time focused on and complaining about what they *don't have* and focused on what they *don't want*, instead of focusing on what they *do want* in their lives.

But that's not you because you are reading this book. You know that if you want change, you have to take action to change. Otherwise there will always be somebody telling you how to run your life, making you feel insecure and doubtful. I know people, as I'm sure you do, who go to work every day to a job that they hate. They hate what they earn and/or what they do, but they stay because they feel they have no other choice. But we all have a choice, and yes the choice may be a difficult one, but you do have a choice.

So to wrap up here are some points to consider as you move forward:

Clarify what is it that you want? What end result are you striving for… and more importantly, Why? What will this objective provide to you? Why you want it will be the driving force.

For now, don't think about whether you *believe* you can accomplish a certain thing or not, just focus on what you *really* want, why you want it, what inspires you. Where do you want to be in one year. Do you want greater freedom in your life, more money, take vacations or spend more time with the family? Do you want to secure your retirement, purchase a new home or automobile?

Close your eyes for a moment and visualize your *ideal* life. If you could live your life on your own terms how would that look and feel to you?

Create a written plan of action. What could you do to today that would take you closer to your goals? How about tomorrow, next week, next month, over the next six months, over the next year? Planning ahead is crucial for success. Review the plan regularly to remind you of what needs to be done. Tweak your plan when necessary. If something isn't working, find new creative ways to move forward. Don't stop. Keep moving forward. Even small steps can make a big difference.

The Change 2

Don't give up. If you meet with challenges that get you down. Get up and dust yourself off and got back to work. You can do it. Keep moving forward.

Make a commitment to yourself. Make a commitment that doesn't allow for anything less. There is no 99% or 110% commitment. A commitment is a promise you make to yourself that you will not stop until the job is done. "I will do no less than whatever it takes to get the job done."

Need help? Ask for it. Don't be a lone ranger. If you find you are overwhelmed and don't know where to turn, ask for help. Hiring a coach is a good place to start - someone that will hold you accountable. Seriously, a coach might be the critical factor in helping you get through your barriers and obstacles. I'm here to help you. That's my mission in life, to help others get what they want.

When interviewing thousands of successful business owners, the one thing that they wish they had done to gain some momentum was to hire a coach. Whether it's me or someone else, a coach can be the catalyst to overcoming the obstacles that might otherwise derail you from achieving your dreams.

Too many people today take their dreams lightly. They make them an alternative instead of an imperative. They put them off until that "someday." Don't wait, because time doesn't.

Achieving great things does not happen if you are not clear and passionate about what you want. Passion is a very important part of the achievement process. Passion lifts your spirit and energizes your heart and mind to moving you faster into a higher level of performance. Passion combined with commitment doesn't allow for struggle, only temporary setbacks. Passion and commitment provide the inspiration and determination to keep moving forward when you hit obstacles or when you face uncertainty.

To Contact Misty:

423-240-0794

MistySuccess@gmail.com

The Change 2

Sarah Jean Aguinaldo

Sarah Jean Aguinaldo is the founder of Lifeward Choices Empowerment Centre. She is skilled in empowering lives and guiding people to discover their life's purpose and experience fulfillment. Aguinaldo is the author of several articles on the most talked about topics amongst LCEC's clients, including success, self-esteem, letting go of pain, being happy and cheating. Her articles along with numerous life enhancing videos are available at SarahAguinaldo.com. Aguinaldo's passions shone through early in life. In 1998, as a teenager, she received the University of Women Award for community development, presented by Member of Parliament, Jean Augustine. Women's Post celebrated Aguinaldo as the *Women of the Week* in Spring 2013 for contributing to individuals' transformation. Aguinaldo pursued an Honors B.A in Environment and Resource Management and Urban, Economic and Social Geography, at the University of Toronto (UofT), and completed her B.Ed. and M.Ed. at the Ontario Institute for Studies in Education at UofT. Her spirituality interests and research began in 2010, deepening in 2011, while healing from an Achilles injury from playing for a women's basketball league. Her healing led her to discover life-changing meditative practices; she shares this knowledge in all of her work, at LCEC, and with everyone she meets.

Consciousness Is The Catalyst For Change

By Sarah Jean Aguinaldo

To realize that Consciousness is the catalyst for Change indicates a profound awakening.

It means you experience the power of being anyone you wish to be

and

having anything you wish to have.

It means you are empowered to seize and create opportunities

that enhance your Being as a whole,

helping you become a more efficient You

in all areas of your life.

LET THE TRUTH OF YOUR BEING INSPIRE YOU TO CHANGE

The time has come to get the maximum results and the highest performing You. This can only come about if you know the whole story - the Truth. To only share some parts for the sake of providing "more practical and concrete information," presupposes that you are not yet capable of, or ready for higher thinking, thus depriving you of valuable empowering knowledge. So, although practical guidelines are certainly easy to grasp and apply, it doesn't mean that out-of-the-box concepts cannot also become such. As you do additional research on ideas emphasized throughout this chapter, remember that the more open you are to going out on a limb to accept certain concepts as true, the faster you can begin experimenting with them, without hesitancy or interfering doubt and thus, discover the biggest, undeniable evidence that will strengthen your beliefs - your inevitable unique evolution. Thus, let's begin to explore the bigger picture, the entire operating system, and this uncovering is, in itself, a rising of CONSCIOUSNESS within you, which is indeed the turbo booster for creating Change in all aspects of your life.

Going straight to the Truth's core:

Personal development is spiritual evolution (Louise, H., 2004).

"I need to become spiritual and holy, in order to improve myself and my life?" you ponder.

No. You cannot become what you already are. You already *are* spiritual. You are a spiritual being having a physical experience (Laura Silva). Take a moment to let that sink in; read this line again. This is an increasingly expressed concept in self-development discourse, as mind-boggling as it initially may be. It's difficult to comprehend, let alone accept, that which we cannot witness with our human eyes. Nevertheless, Dr. Konstantin Korotkov, a Professor of Physics at Saint Petersburg University, helps us do just that with his invention of Electrophotonic Imaging (EPI). EPI technique is a real-time viewing of humans' energy fields.

"We are not just material beings; we are not just flesh. We are much more than that - we are energy beings, we are light beings... we are Divine Light," Korotkov expresses.

Also, according to quantum field theorists, human bodies are made up of atoms that are made up of subatomic particles which, in turn, are fluctuations of energy and information (Chopra, D., 1998). Thus, the personal growth process is about enhancing what is already within you!

It is the spiritual You that seeks self-development and lifestyles that are more healthy, joyous, peaceful and collaborative. The spiritual You wants to be better, feel better, look better, have improved relationships, and overall, do and achieve more in this lifetime.

"So, if I want more money, then I'm being *spiritual*? If I'm training for bigger muscles, then I'm being *spiritual*?" you ask in puzzlement.

If it reflects and is representative of self-love - yes! Self-development/spiritual evolution is LOVE FOR SELF in action! The spiritual self is naturally comprised of Love energy, which explains any desires to care for and give to your being. It explains why you want to help yourself live the best life possible! Can you see it? Your interest in Change is an expression of self-love, as are all the things you are currently doing and will do to help bring about the most meaningful Change in your life, such as reading this book.

CHOOSE SELF-LOVE AND COME ALIVE

Thus, self-love is a key determinant of your overall success in experiencing Change as well as in maintaining Change throughout your life. Why? It is the fuel for your evolution. It keeps you passionately engaged in your developmental process as you CONSCIOUSLY fulfill a unique life purpose. Self-love ensures you're pursuing self-improvement based on your heart's desires, and not on intellectual or logical decisions, which often only fulfill *someone else's* criteria of happiness.

Before exploring the life-changing chain reactions of self-love, first familiarize yourself with the FEELING of self-love, so that you can CONSCIOUSLY recognize it, open to it, choose it and make it the new norm in your life. Fill up on this fuel in preparation for your upcoming journey! Creatively indulge in the blissful experience of self-love in as many ways as you can possibly think of. What does self-love look like to you?

Perhaps pamper yourself with spa and massage experiences. Give thanks for beautification; become addicted to relaxation. Write down all your talents and past achievements - read them often and praise yourself each time for your greatness. Acknowledge how far you've come! Exercise and stretch in front of a mirror on a regular basis; enjoy supporting yourself and witnessing your transformation. Connect deeply with positive affirmations, prayers, and mantras. Recite them regularly and keep these loving phrases at the forefront of your mind throughout your day.

Listen to various meditations - guided or frequency-based, self-love focused or other, and let the energy of the words and sounds penetrate your being. Let the undeniable vibrations and tingles you feel throughout your physical body be proof that your energy is changing during meditation. You'll also want to smile and laugh for no particular reason, for many hours after the meditation is done! Inner joy is the loving result!

The key is to experiment with different things and see what resonates with you. Take your time in the moment of each act and tune into how it makes you feel. Then, create opportunities for yourself to engage in the ones that make you feel absolutely wonderful as often as you can.

CONSCIOUSLY bask in the pleasure. This is the start of loving life, feeling so good to be here. You become more CONSCIOUS of your existence and of the power you have to make yourself feel alive! You deserve it!

EXPERIENCE QUALITY LIVING

As the love energy builds within you, it must be released and will burst forth in all directions… quenching and nurturing all areas of your life, causing Change of all kinds. For instance, when you love yourself, you inevitably think about your health. You CONSCIOUSLY think about what you are putting into your body. Ask yourself if a particular food choice will do something helpful or harmful to your physique, cells, and organs, and choose accordingly. Do you want to go to the gym, join a sports team, or perhaps do yoga to supplement your new eating habits? How far can you take this? Are you curious?

When you love yourself, you cannot tolerate harmful or disrespectful interactions. You know how wonderful you are, and that you're worthy of healthy relations. You naturally seek and attract such, and swiftly disengage from relationships at all levels – friendships and romantic partnerships - that do not fit in with your beliefs about how you deserve to be treated. You love how caring people make you feel; you set the bar and expect this always. As a result, the people in your life who you are very close to are nothing short of amazing!

When you love yourself, stress, worry, and sadness do not stay with you for long. You refuse to wallow in hardships and instead, recognize what others call "horrific problems" as opportunities for self-growth. You see your "obstacles" as chances to switch life paths and travel towards destinies that you weren't headed for otherwise. You don't miss a beat, and as soon as an issue arises, you CONSCIOUSLY choose to take action and problem-solve. There's no time to feel anxious, nervous, or cry for much longer since you're underway with making everything better, making life great. Thus, you know the hurdles are there for a reason; you need them now to evolve and so, you are grateful for them. You embrace them.

FULFILL YOUR HEART'S DESIRES THROUGH THE POWER OF THOUGHT

By filling up on love as described above, you become the elixir guaranteed to give rise to success, financial wealth, healing, joy and anything your heart desires. This is because your thoughts create your reality (Chopra, D., 2004), and self-love ensures you have thoughts of fulfilling personal dreams. Like a parent nurturing a child, you want to support yourself to land the job you want, make sure you have more than enough money, see yourself fall in love, praise yourself as you pursue your passions, and overall, help yourself to simply be yourself and happy in all ways. So, get specific and design your life in detail, visualizing and imagining yourself living the life you want to live, and having and doing all the things you want to have and do. These thoughts will become your reality. You can change your life.

"In other words, just focus and keep my eye on the prize?" you ask. "Follow the *work hard pays off* motto?"

Once you grasp how much more it is than the above concepts, you can more CONSCIOUSLY and thus, more consistently and effectively navigate through the creation process with precision and personalized intent and excitement. Returning to this chapter's opening discussion of your spiritual-energy self, realize that your thoughts, which is information, contribute to your energy and your makeup. So, not only are you the energy of Light, Spirit, and Love, you are also the energy of Consciousness. You ARE Consciousness. You are like words and information swirling around in infinite combinations and patterns making the shape of your physical body (Deepak, C., 1998)! Therefore, the creative force and energy that Consciousness is (in the basic sense), flows in the direction your thoughts send it, molding and shaping your thought patterns into other energies - into physical forms in the physical world. Consequently, you see what your thoughts look like in the reality around you. Once again, your thoughts create your reality. Hence the importance of infusing your being with love as previously discussed; a negative state of being would produce negative realities, and a positive state of being shall produce positive realities.

To help you further contemplate the invisible thought - visible reality relationship, consider the fact that "everything is in geometrical relationship to everything else creating energetic patterns" (Marciniak, B., 1995). Jason Padgett even developed the prodigious ability, after suffering a brain injury, to see everything around him in terms of geometry. He sees angles and shapes everywhere, "from the geometry of a rainbow, to the fractals in water spiraling down a drain" (Lewis, T., 2014). Researchers continue to study his brain and his new abilities to draw genius mathematical drawings of what he sees. Thus, be CONSCIOUS of the fact that what you put out is what you get back.

DISCOVER INNER PEACE

There may be lapses in your Change journey but if you are CONSCIOUS of the point you are coming from, CONSCIOUS while you travel, and CONSCIOUS of the point you are moving towards, you can better monitor your progress, recognize when you're off-track and more easily understand what needs to be done to reach your destination. Therefore, clearly identify what you no longer want in your life; identify what you want instead. Identify what you no longer want to act like; identify the new you that you shall now emanate. Having this map makes finding the treasure easier!

Where do you start? Make lifeward choices - choices that make your life drama-free, bring you inner peace, and make your heart smile. They encourage you to let go of past issues that do not benefit you in any way. They help you forgive people and realize they acted to the best of their knowledge. Lifeward choices push you to move on with a new life and new you. This may not, of course, be the easiest thing to begin, especially if you've spent many years doing the opposite, but this is when you need to turn that self-love on *high* - believe in yourself and encourage yourself. Also, when negative situations persist amidst your positivity, don't give up. Rather, let them act as precious alarms warning you to clear out old beliefs and energies from your being. You need to figure out why you are still bonded to things that cause pain or stress. Do you really believe alternatives cannot nourish and love you better? Do you want to clear this from your system or not? Do you really want Change?

When you commit to self-development, you will eventually find that your world is less chaotic and quieter, both outside and within you. Remember - your inner energy creates your external energy. Thus, there's nothing to stress about nowadays. You only think of the *things-to-do* when you briefly open your agenda. There's no one to worry about because you know everyone's responsible for their happiness, and you send them blessings for peace. There's no one to fight with; the people you spend time with are sources of laughter and hugs. There's nothing to doubt or hope for, since self-love always gets you what you want.

You never knew there was so much time in a day to watch the clouds float by slowly, to watch flocks of birds make pretty designs across the sky, to see tree branches dance to various beats, and to enjoy the breeze on your face. You even have time to realize how thankful you are for this moment. You realize how thankful you are for your life, for nature, for all the things you have, for all the people you know, for all the great things that happened earlier today, yesterday, and the day before that. It's time to acknowledge that you are Spirit, Light, Love, Consciousness, Serenity and Gratitude. These energies are interconnected and build upon each other.

Thus, you give thanks for You. You enjoy You. You increasingly tune into You. Your quieter and calm world makes this easier. You find yourself attracted to meditative practices that help enhance this newfound relationship with Self. Most of your meditations are with closed eyes and in private spaces; yet, you realize that you can feel the same loving vibrations and inner connection, regardless of where you are, with eyes wide-open. You realize this in line at the movies, driving your car, in a crowded mall, while you deliver a presentation, and so on. You are CONSCIOUS of yourself, of your essence. This is a new Change within you.

RECEIVE DIVINE GUIDANCE

This Change within you also means you can recognize vibrations other than your own. You increasingly become aware of surrounding frequencies - other energies, entities, and consciousnesses of nonphysical places or dimensions. You *feel* your connection to Source. This presence is undeniable.

Personal development or spiritual evolution means your energy level is enhanced and thus, you begin to associate with other spiritually evolved energies. This will include a mix of humans here on earth and nonphysical energies from beyond, like Angels, Ascended Masters, and other cosmic beings. This all leads to an overall deepening connection with Source. The experiential knowledge and proof of such will be yours when you get there!

I've only recently reached this spot myself and only just begun exploring the surface of this amazing adventure. Nevertheless, one thing's for sure - the loving support of surrounding energies, and the loving support of Source are available. They've always been here, within us, without us, but now, we can be CONSCIOUS of such. Now, we can actively merge and unite with Source, not only at times of prayer, but with every waking moment, and thus, we are guided to infuse love into every life decision and act.

Everything we ask help with, we receive. Hence, I am thankful for the help I received to express the knowledge in this chapter that I share with you.

Be CONSCIOUS of this Divine Guidance and welcome it. Answers and information for support will come to you through conversations with strangers or close friends, in dreams, or "coincidently" pop up in a documentary you watch or in an article you read. Opportunities will present themselves to you, left, right and centre. Be empowered by this help and go forth without fear, knowing that you are not alone in your pursuit of Change. The Divine is with you always.

CHANGE CONSCIOUSLY

Consciousness is the catalyst for Change. Regularly reflect on your personal development experiences and make appropriate adjustments. This ensures engagement; you are a Creator of Change in your life.

Be aware of the energies that comprise your being, and how you give rise to or hinder them.

Be aware of which life areas you focus on and which ones you neglect.

Be aware of the reasons behind seeking fulfillment of certain life purposes.

Be aware of your feelings, emotions and thoughts.

Be aware of inner energies creating external realities.

Be aware of your choices of action or inaction.

Be aware of progress and your associated reactions.

Be aware of how you collaborate with others to reach personal goals.

Be aware with your relationship with Source.

Realize that you are here, right where you need to be.

I praise you for wanting betterment and Change.

I send you much love and support upon your journey.

To Contact Sarah:

sarah@sarahaguinaldo.com

sarah@lifewardchoices.com

1-888-290-1888 Extension 700

sarahaguinaldo.com

lifewardchoices.com

facebook.com/LifewardChoicesEmpowermentCentre

instagram.com/sarahaguinaldo

sarahaguinaldo on Instagram

sarah_aguinaldo on Twitter

womenspost.ca/women-of-the-week-sarah-jean-aguinaldo/

lifeinsights.guru

REFERENCES

Chopra, Deepak. (1998). Creat*ing Affluence: The A-to-Z Steps to a Richer Life*. California: Amber-Allen

Publishing and New World Library.

Chopra, Deepak. (2003). *The Spontaneous Fulfillment of Desire: Harnessing the Infinite Power of Coincidence*. USA: The Three Rivers Press.

Hay, Louise L. (2004). *You Can Heal Your Life*. USA: Hay House, Inc.

Korotkov, Dr.Konstantin. Official Website. Available at: http://www.korotkov.eu/

Lewis, Tanya. (May 5, 2014). *"A Beautiful Mind: Brain Injury Turns Man into Math Genius."*

Available at http://m.livescience.com/45349-brain-injury-turns-man-into-math-genius.html

Marciniak, Barbara. (1995). *Earth: Pleiadian Keys to the Living Library*. USA: Inner Traditions Bear & Company, Inc.

Silva, Laura. *"How to Develop Intuition."* Available at

http://s3.amazonaws.com/silvalifesystem/intuition/How-to-Develop-Intuition.pdf

The Change 2

Shannon Graham

Shannon Graham is Visionary Mentor who specializes in leadership development and peak performance for high achievers. For over ten years, Shannon has worked with leaders from all walks of life - from athletes, millionaires, non-profits, single mothers, and everyone in-between. His breakthrough trainings include The Ultimate Lifestyle intensive, a highly popular weekend immersion program, and Legacy Shannon's high-level twelve month program. His coaching is not for the faint of heart.

Visionary Leadership

Shannon Graham

Leadership as we know it must die. The current state of the world is a great mirror for where our existing levels of leadership have gotten us. Pollution, war, and disease have become an epidemic worldwide. Personal gain has greatly outweighed social responsibility. There must be a conscious decision to adopt new beliefs about what leadership is, and what it is not. For too long, we have subscribed to the idea that leadership is about force and domination. The current paradigm of leadership is one dimensional and gives people a misconstrued idea of what leadership really is. As a result, our water is becoming undrinkable, the air is becoming unbreathable, and our food inedible. Yet the monster far greater than the one we have unleashed on the world is the plague of indifference we have unleashed on our people. Much of the world has adopted a "whatever" attitude and it is clearly demonstrated in our youth. In order for the problems at hand to be powerfully solved, we must create a new example of leadership to inspire the generation who's job it is to clean up the mess we have made. I call this…

Visionary Leadership

I define visionary leadership as this:

The ability to clearly see a specific desired outcome while inspiring others unto your movement by embodying its legacy.

With our brief time here together, I will be outlining the two major myths of leadership, the key personality traits of a Visionary Leader, understanding your gift, and the actions you can take to be a part of the shift needed to change the world as we know it. But first, a story about my origin as a visionary leader…

I was always the quiet type, never did anything too rash or our of the norm. Everything went according to plan for the most part, and there was never any reason to be radical. One day that all changed. I was at school and we were playing one of my all time favorite games… capture the flag. To me it was not a game, it was life and death. It was a challenge to see what I was truly made of. This one game in particular was a disaster, no - it was a massacre. One by one I saw my teammates being sent to jail, their valiant efforts in vain. With only a few of us left, the outcome looked bleak. Suddenly I was struck with a glorious vision. It was me leading my team to a righteous victory after a daring jailbreak. If you are not familiar, in capture the flag you can perform what is called a "jailbreak," where you must run into the enemy territory… and if you reach the jail untagged, you may set all of those in jail free. I no longer heard the loud cries of my teammates, all I could hear was a resounding roar from the depths of my soul.

At that moment. timid Shannon did not exist. The need for radical action had arrived and I was the one chosen to lead the charge. I crouched and sprang forward with an indomitable spirit unafraid of the immense danger on the other side. As I crossed the threshold, one word erupted from the depths of my being… "JAILBREAK." As I plunged into the heart of darkness, each adversary was met with unrelenting resolve and quickness of step. Agile and determined, I out-ran and out-maneuvered each and every person. The faces of the captured - both shocked and in awe - came alive with the promise of another shot at victory. Together we crossed back into our home territory with renewed spirits.

We won the game that day and my vision was realized. I tell you that story to set the stage for the first myth we must bust in leadership.

Leadership Myths

Myth #1 Leaders are born, not made.

My story is a perfect example of the opposite of this. I never had any desire to lead or belief that I could. However, circumstance changed all of that and I became in that moment, something I never knew I had the power to be. Society tends to only show the highlight reel of leaders, making us believe that they have always been bold, amazing leaders. This is far from the truth. That is similar to saying that every professional athlete naturally had their ability to perform in sports all along. Greatness in any field is gained, not inherited.

This is truly a tragedy in our world because many of those who have the potential to be great leaders feel like they cannot be, because they never have been before. Which is like deciding to not do anything simply because you never have. There is a difference between what you have done in the past and what you have the potential to do now. The limits of our potential are only just barely being understood, the one major factor at the core of that understanding is… there are no limits.

If you observe great leaders you will see that they are forged out of necessity. Their belief in their cause gives them the ability to see the invisible and do the impossible. They were ordinary men and women who did extraordinary things. This means that if being a leader is a part of your destiny, no lack of experience will matter.

Leaders are made by a burning desire and definiteness of purpose; past experience is not needed.

Myth #2 Leaders must always be at the front.

The iconic pictures painted of leadership include things like a King Leonidas leading his faithful 300 into battle. It is believed that leaders must always remain at the forefront. However, again because of how leaders are portrayed, what you do not see is how they also remove themselves and reflect. For a leader, having time to reconnect with their vision, strength, and alignment are crucial. Especially in a world that is driven by performance, the idea of stopping to take time to unplug is not common.

A leader must be responsible for seeing their vision into fruition. This means that burnout, though rampant in our culture, is not an option. The world does not benefit from a dream half realized. There is a timing required, a certain cadence needed in order to successfully dance with destiny. Leonidas did not simply charge his men into battle, he planned and prepared. It was in his down time that he created what is still talked about to this day as one of the greatest war strategies of all time.

To successfully lead you must be sure to remove yourself from the forefront in order to cultivate your genius.

Key Traits of Visionary Leadership.

Now let us turn our attention on the most fundamental aspect of leadership. In a world that is focused primarily on "how" to do things, the overlooked ingredient is "who" you must become in order to powerfully lead. Tips, tricks, and tools are useless, unless you have the personal power to implement those things. This is why the "who" is infinitely more important than the "how." The following are the key personality traits of Visionary Leadership.

Vision - This one may seem obvious however, this is the core of what a leader moves and breathes from. Thus, you must challenge yourself to see your vision with even more clarity, height, and width.

How will you know when your dream has been realized?

What is the major transformation that will happen as a result of your movement?

What is the tyranny your cause fights against?

Visionary leaders thrive when they have clarity. Spend as much time as needed vetting your vision. The more clearly and boldly you can feel your vision, the easier it will be to stay inspired as well as inspire others to follow you.

Passion - There is a certain magnetism that comes with high levels of passion. Every leader who plans to make a serious difference in the world must have it. Passion is a large part of what ignites others to get behind your movement.

What is it about your vision that lights your soul on fire?

How can you blend your enthusiasm into your communication?

How can you continue to fan the flame of your passion?

Structure - One of the biggest challenges for those with big visions is that they think too much. They have so many ideas bouncing around in their mind that it becomes paralyzed. Clarity helps with this but, there must also be structure. Structure means two things in this context.

#1 Structure means discipline. So many would-be leaders fall short of their legacy because they do not have the discipline needed to stay on a straight and narrow path to success. Discipline gives a visionary the boundaries that are necessary to maintain focus and continuously make progress. This means you must understand your own Personal Patterns of Excellence, which is your own personal criteria for greatness. We all have certain rituals and habits that allow us to thrive. The idea is to figure out how you, as an individual, operate at the highest level and create a discipline of doing those specific things each day.

#2 Structure also means external systems. This generally takes the shape of having a team and an infrastructure that allows for that team to thrive. Many organizations are finding that creating structure has less to do with hard rules to follow, and strict protocols, and more to do with creating an environment of excellence. This means sharing your vision with your team, giving them goals and objectives to meet, and also allowing them the ability to let their personal powers of creativity and ingenuity to thrive.

If structure is the foundation for progress, how solid is the structure you currently have?

How much would you benefit from increasing your personal discipline?

What systems or people do you have in place currently, to help support you?

Innovation - As a Visionary Leader you must push the boundaries of what is possible. You must not only be a dreamer, you must also be a pioneer. We must continue to improve the examples of radical leadership in the world. Our greatest moments of legacy must not be behind us. This means that you must be willing to go to the edge of what is known, and what is safe, in order to go beyond.

Innovation means that you must constantly work on developing your own creative powers. You must expand your capacity to improve that which you see.

How can you challenge yourself to think outside of the box?

What is currently in place that would benefit from innovation?

How can you think even more creatively?

Personal Power - Being a leader is not as easy as having a vision and sharing it with the world. Leading a movement is taxing in every sense of the word. You must fortify yourself mentally, emotionally, and spiritually, in order to expand your capacity to take on the challenges of being a leader. Inspiration alone is not enough, there must be mental toughness. Every great leader throughout history has faced great adversity, and without an indomitable spirit, their dreams would have never been realized. Increasing mental toughness breaks down into dedicating yourself to constant and never ending improvement. This requires you to have the ability to control your emotions, self motivate, maintain a positive attitude, and live beyond your comfort zone.

What are you currently doing to protect your vision through investing in the development of yourself and those entrusted to help lead your movement?

Which of the following areas are you weakest: Emotional control? Self motivation? Maintaining a positive attitude? Pushing beyond your comfort zone?

Are you currently working with a coach to help you improve these areas?

Hard Work - Yes, good old fashioned hard work. Rome, my friend, was not built in a day. And guess what? Nothing truly worthwhile is either. To realize your dream, you must roll up your sleeves and be willing to wake up early and stay up late. At this time in history, hard work is all but forgotten. Most people believe that hard work is no longer needed because we can now "work smarter." Nothing could be further from the truth. Of course you should work smart, but there is something invaluable about having a strong work ethic. Have you ever noticed how many of those who have gained great fortune by working their ass off, are perceived as being lucky or special? Funny enough, those who perceive successful people that way, often believe a similar "luck" will befall them and their lives will instantly change. Blood, sweat, and tears will always be prime ingredients for growing a dream.

You must do the work. YOU as the LEADER... MUST... DO... the... WORK.

Is there hard work you are avoiding?

Are you willing to work harder than ever before?

Do you have examples in your past where you have worked hard?

Understand Your Gift

There are two types of people in the world. The first are people who HAVE a gift. These are the artists and craftsmen of the world. They literally create things to bring forward for the world to utilize - Thomas Edison, Nikola Tesla, Henry Ford, to name a few examples. Modern day examples include Elon Musk, Steve Jobs, and Tony Hsieh. The second type of people ARE the gift. This means, by being in the atmosphere, there is an energetic transfer, and those on the receiving end are leveled up. These are people like Jesus, Gandhi, and Martin Luther King Jr. Modern examples are people such as Oprah, Thich Nhat Hanh, and Shannon Graham.

The Change 2

As a leader, you must have clarity about which you are, out of these two. Having clarity in this area helps you understand how to best bring forth your gift. This clarity also brings with it a level of responsibility. By that I mean, whatever your gift is, it is meant to be brought forth in a way that has the highest probability of transformation for those whom it is meant for. This is where often, we must let go of our ego and transcend what "we" want and look at the big picture of how best we can serve others with our gift. Our vision must go far beyond us and our lifetime. The ego seeks to be a great distraction. Praise, monuments, and fame must be let go of. It is this level of altruism that allows us to move past transactions and remain focused on transformation.

We live in a world that is highly focused on leverage and automation; it is very reliant on technology to accomplish this. Though technology has allowed those who HAVE a gift to easily and powerfully bring it forth to the world, technology has damaged those who ARE the gift. The simple reason is because as soon as you try to leverage or automate someone who IS the gift, you instantly separate the gift from the person and dramatically dilute the gift. A popular belief in the success and self-help industry is that you must get your message in front of as many people as possible. On paper, this idea makes sense, however, my counter question would be... At the end of the day, how many people were truly transformed by your work?

Getting your "message" in front of millions does not change the world. Transforming people does. The reality is, Jesus did not perform miracles on millions of people, he only was face to face with a small handful of people of whom received his gifts. This is where the limiting belief must be broken. We must remember that changing the world of one person is enough. We must know that anything other than our best method for delivering our gift, robs those who are intended to be served by it.

My prediction is that creating intimate experiences where others can be exposed to another's gifts first hand, will become the core of how we engage. Technology has removed the human element from the equation of daily life, and thus taken away the magic that comes from being in an environment of excellence. We learn at the highest level via experience; it is the most real and visceral way we move through life. As we reach a point where emotionally we are bankrupt and visually we are over-stimulated with texts, tweets, updates, emails, and Instagram, we will come full circle. We will no longer use technology as the vehicle to experience life through, rather it will be used as a bridge where we will connect with others and transfer from the internet to real life.

The reason you are still reading these words is clear. YOU are meant to be a visionary leader and make a drastic difference in the world. And whether you have a gift or you are the gift, I promise you the world needs the transformation you can bring it. My wish for you is to unleash your true potential so that you can lead your movement with a level of clarity and power like never before. The cost of inaction is too high and the gifts you have been given are too valuable to waste. There will never be a better time for greatness than now. I encourage you to reach out to me if you feel called to explore working together.

Go forth, be great.

Shannon

To Contact Shannon:

www.thementorcoach.com

www.shannongraham.com

The Change 2

Stephanie Ann Gamble

Stephanie Ann Gamble is a natural born leader, motivator, and mentor. She thrives on helping others, self-mastery, and living a life of purpose and abundance. She truly believes that everyone deserves a life of abundance and we can all achieve our excellent life.

Stephanie has always enjoyed inspiring others through her works as an accomplished platform artist in the beauty industry, an award winning stylist, a professional mentor, and a successful business owner/manager. She has also been an empowering Human Resource leader where employee relations and motivation are key.

In 2013, Stephanie began a Professional Coaching program by IPEC. Through this program, all of her knowledge and hands on experience in life was be put together and shared with all who agree that life is full of abundance.

Stephanie holds a PHD in life; Personal Human Development. This is something we all hold, however the difference is what we choose to do with it. We all go through the motions in life, why not have fun, be fabulous and live your excellent life!

Build your mind, reframe your thoughts, and live your most excellent life!

By Stephanie Gamble

We are truly amazing creatures, every one of us, and we are equipped with a magnificent thing we call our mind. The mind is full of thoughts, stories, beliefs, and values. Within these minds, we create our future, relive our past, and influence the entire world around us. We have the ability to influence everything with which we make contact. We make life choices and foster relationships with others and ourselves. We take action or hold back, based on what is on and in our mind. The mind is a truly powerful tool, a tool to be developed and to be used to fulfill our purpose and create our destiny. Yet most of us spend our time obsessing over our bodies, our weight, our looks, and even our material worth. Since our mind influences everything we do, as well as all of our choices and relationships, it only makes sense that we lend more time to building a more positive, supportive, and more powerful mind.

When I was a teen, I read my first motivational/inspirational book called *The Power of Positive Thinking*, by Norman Vincent Peale. I had just left high school, where so much emphasis was placed on physical looks. I was in constant turmoil of being a "heavy girl" and welcomed a fresh approach to life. I became amazed at the power of our thoughts as I practiced the activities in Peale's book. I was amazed that a simple positive statement could reframe my thinking. This positive statement could change my attitude and support my actions toward achieving my goals. It was this moment when I began my journey of using affirmations as triggers for reducing stress, keeping forward momentum toward my goals and for overall happiness. I began filling my mind with words of encouragement, peace, and positivity.

I continued to read books, take seminars and listen to tapes. I began to realize that building one's mind and framing one's thoughts to support the authentic and true self was a key component to achieving the life that I had set out to attain. When I encountered challenges or adverse opinions and roadblocks, the value of positive thinking, framing, reframing and mind building became transparent. I began framing new thoughts of success and reframing thoughts that do not support me. I was building an optimistic and confident mind that would allow prosperity in my life.

Understanding thoughts

Thoughts, statements, opinions, and events are encountered every day, and frame conscious choices and actions that ultimately shape our day and life. Many of those thoughts, statements, opinions, and events are developed by conscious values, or values that are based on fear, worry, and doubt. The "I should" or the "I need to" thoughts and actions are examples of conscious-based values. Those thoughts and actions are usually founded on limited beliefs or assumptions that are not fully aligned with one's core values.

Limited beliefs are belief systems that have been imposed by an outside source like family members, a boss, or society. In some cases, we adopt parts of these values as our own. However, in the instance of the "I should" or the "I need" thought, I encourage everyone to question the alignment of core values. For example, a limiting belief may be that all work must be done before thinking of fun. Since "a woman's work is never done," fun might just have to wait until another day. If one's core value is to allow yourself down time, then this limiting belief conflicts with your core value and blocks one from living a fulfilling life. In fact, following this limiting belief may evoke a place of discontent and frustration, which are both energy-depleting emotions. Reframing this thought to a more balanced approach of - a little fun fit into a little work, is what works best for most. It may even launch one's energy to a new level. Reframing thoughts based on limiting beliefs will remove the barriers or walls, which can improve energy and allow one to live a most excellent life.

Assumptions are the statements which we tell ourselves to be true, and are based on what has happened in the past. Therefore, we assume that when we engage in a situation, we already know what the outcome will be. As with limiting beliefs, assumptions can be safety mechanisms that are set in place to keep us from harm. This may be true for several things, as not touching a hot stove because it will cause a burn, or not applying for another management position because you have been turned down twice. Before making an assumption, I encourage looking into one's core value or purpose, and then make the choice based on the decision that aligns with one's authentic self. In other words, if one's goal and purpose is to attain a management level position, reframing the thought or assumption will be key to supporting goals and purpose. That reframed thought might look like, "When the timing is right and the position is right for me, I am confident that I will be selected for the job." The consequences of not reframing that thought or not taking action will result in not attaining the goal. Remember, every individual has the power and the choice to frame their thoughts, actions, and lives in a way that serves and supports their goals and purpose to live their most excellent lives.

The Art of Reframing

Reframing is the single most important and easy activity that can be completed to influence and change one's future and life. Reframing is the art of taking a thought, sentence, idea, fear, worry, doubt, or limited belief, and changing it to support goals, values, and one's life journey. Think of a carpenter who has been contracted to remodel a house, a task that includes building a wall between two rooms. If the carpenter frames the wall to span from floor to ceiling, the purpose for the wall might be to act as a supporting structure for that ceiling. Alternatively, the wall's purpose could solely be to separate each room so that each room has a unique purpose. That wall serves a purpose that the carpenter or homeowner chose for it. What if the carpenter builds the wall from floor to ceiling and then realizes that closing off each room does not fully serve the purpose, perhaps eliminating sunlight, which is a high core value of the owner? Then the carpenter can reframe the wall to begin at the floor, but end half way up the room. This setup still adds a separation between the two living spaces, and lets the sunlight in, fulfilling that value of the homeowner. I have used this analogy because most people walk through life taking walls for granted. People bump into them, move around them, or turn back and deal with them as if there is not any alternative. Everyone has the ability to reframe all the walls in life into supporting structures and statements that let all the light of purpose and abundance into their world. Reframing is a simple, yet powerful tool.

The art of reframing is as easy as it sounds. As described above, it is the art of taking a statement and restructuring it to support one's goal and purpose. An integral part of reframing is to begin by becoming aware or taking notice of the current thoughts that are affecting choices and influencing energy. It starts with what currently fills the mind. In many cases, people are not aware of the negative thoughts or statements they are encountering since they have become an autonomic response. For example, when waking in the morning, a common and instant thought that goes through one's mind is "I do not want to get up," and the snooze button is pressed once or twice. Another response might be "aww, it's still dark out." These statements are neither right nor wrong, and for the most part, pointing out the negative point of view is human nature. In fact, most negative thoughts come from the safety net that has been developed, or has been instilled deep inside each of us, by limited beliefs and assumptions. All of this negative programming has people looking for what is wrong, or the downside of a situation, rather than the positive upside, gratitude, and/or beauty of the situation or element. It is easy for one to come up with the negative thoughts and it takes more work to create positive thoughts. This speaks to the conscious values of fear, doubt, and worry... the "I should" or "I shouldn't" and "I need to" concepts. Hitting the snooze button while saying or thinking "I do not want to get up," might refer negative feelings associated with the need to go to work. Now take a moment to think about your reaction to the alarm when your thoughts are "I love my work and am excited to get up and go.. Would it be more similar to the feelings people have when they rise out of bed on the morning of the day they are leaving for vacation? People generally do not hit the snooze button or make any groans of discontent when filled with excitement to get up for such occasions. The more aligned your thoughts are with your goals, values, and purpose, the more energy and excitement there is in your world. So once again, I want to stress, the first step you need to take is to be aware of your current thoughts. Use this awareness and then take the step to promote thoughts that align with goals, values, and purpose. In the morning, reframe any of those negative thoughts to, "it's a bright new day," or "I am thankful that I can hit snooze one more time." Try it and see how the day unfolds.

Regarding the effects of energy - negative energy is very depleting. Negative energy drains you and promotes blinders, so that all the possibilities ahead are not seen or realized. As a quick exercise, say the words "I can't" out loud. Notice the energy leave your lungs, and the feeling of the restriction of your chest as the statement is finished. Now state, "yes, I can." Notice the breath fill the lungs and then expand the chest. It is as if energy fills the body. Each time a negative thought appears, practice turning the energy around and stating it in the positive, present tense. Practice taking a deep breath of air while stating the positive reframed thought aloud. Notice the elevated energy, the feeling of being lifted up, and sense of action throughout the body. Reframing thoughts activates and energizes the body and uplifts the spirit. This practice will provide positive energy throughout the day and the entire journey of life. By removing negative energy, the blinders are removed, eyes open wide, and you can begin to see all that life has in store for you.

Being aware of thoughts and recognizing the limiting language that one says to one's self on a daily, hourly, and sometimes minute basis, is the first step to reframing the future. Unfortunately, 60% of that self-talk is negative and is in fact, far worse than words that we would ever say to anyone else. Many of us are so programmed with negative messages to ourselves that these messages have become second nature. They are said both outwardly and internally without effort. How many times have you called yourself an idiot or said, "that was stupid." Each time one says or thinks something that is limiting, negative, or not supportive, we must stop. We must ask how this can be reframed to be positive and supportive. Each time you hear yourself say "I can't" or "I should" or "I need to," pause and change the words to "I can" or "I want to." Each time you call yourself a negative name, reframe it with a positive "I am" statement. I like to use "I am God's beautiful creature."

Reframing our thoughts simply takes a little practice, and one practice that can help to reframe is to write those limiting unsupportive words or thoughts on a piece of paper or note card. Then, either fold or flip the paper over and write the positive alternates of those words or thoughts. For instance, one side of the note card might state, "I am always making mistakes," and the reframed statement on the other side may be, "I enjoy challenges and grow from any mistakes that I make." This positive reframed statement gives permission to make those mistakes, while growing and enjoying life. Another example is that one can also take any statement such as, "I need to lose twenty pounds," write that on one side of a note card and then flip that over and write a positive supportive statement such as, "I want to lose twenty pounds and feel more confident."

Another important component to help with reframing thoughts to is to be curious about one's self. When a thought or statement appears such as, "I cannot" or "I should," ask why. Why should it be or why can't it be? A common business tool is called the Five Whys tool, which is used to get to a root cause analysis. Meaning that by asking why five times, a conclusion will be met as to what caused the action or circumstance. This is an interesting exercise and when used similarly in reframing thoughts and connecting them to core values, it is clarifying and inspiring. The key is to ask why as many times as it takes to uncover a thought that supports goals, value and feels authentic.

An example using the Five Whys tool:

Initial thought: "I should lose twenty pounds".

Why should I lose twenty pounds? "Because I am over weight."

Why do I think I am over weight? "Because my clothes are tight."

Why are my clothes too tight? "Because I do not exercise and I like to eat."

Why do I think exercise is important? "Because it helps burn calories, will tone my body, and then I can still enjoy eating."

Why is exercising important to you obtaining your goal? "I will lose weight, tone my body, and my clothes will not be tight."

Reframed thought: "I want to join a gym, start exercising, and feel great in my clothes."

"Why" can be asked as many times as it takes to get to a thought or statement that feels authentic. Authentic thoughts come from the core, gut, or deep down. These kinds of thoughts are immediately recognizable since they are accompanied by an energy that comes on like a light switch and instantly lifts spirits, evokes solutions and action. This exercise resembles the little child that keeps asking why each time they receive an answer. It is fun, exploratory and amazing what one can end up with. In the example above, the original thought was focused on the twenty pounds and an "I should" statement, which may have been a number imposed by someone else's scale or limiting belief. However, after being curious and using the Five Whys exercise, the realization that focusing on joining a gym and exercising links the values, and now the "should" becomes the "I want to" in order to reach the goal.

Be curious by continuing to keep asking questions and digging deeper into the core to find out what one really wants and values. In addition to asking why, be curious and ask who, what, when, where, and how. "How will that support me?" "What is another way to think of that?" "When is a good time to start?" "Where am I in the process?" By asking these questions, many components of one's self will be uncovered that might otherwise be blinded by those limiting beliefs or assumptions mentioned earlier. In order to live one's most abundant and prosperous life, one must become as familiar and authentic with one's values as possible, and frame thoughts, beliefs and action around them.

Reframed Thoughts

Reframed thoughts are present tense, focused, believable and powerful. Present tense means that these statements are formed with words such as "I am" and "I have." This creates the positive energy of success. The more positive energy is produced, the more positive energy you attract. That is the law of attraction. To be focused, the statement must hone in on the specific goal with as much detail as possible. Many times people will stay large and non-specific to allow room for error. But if we do not keep our eye on the ball, how can we hit it out of the park? One can state "I want to earn a good salary," or one can state "I am earning $100,000 per year." The first statement gives room for the definition of good salary to change. In this instance, one might cope with or settle with less than $100,000, which is a choice that everyone has. However, if one sets their goal as earning $100,000, and keeps their eye on that ball, all our choices and thoughts will focus on "I earn $100,000 per year," and hit it out of the park! So, do not settle, stay focused and keep those thoughts framed around that specific goal. For the thoughts to be believable, one must believe that the reframed thought is achievable. The thought must be attainable. Often times, aggressive goals are set, which are doubted from the beginning. If one starts out with doubt, then our energy starts to deplete. Why not keep energy high with thoughts of success and belief in one's self? Finally and most importantly, reframed thoughts are powerful statements that contain powerful words, and when stated aloud have strength and inspiration. In fact, those reframed thoughts and statements that are stated aloud evoke huge amounts of energy within, physically, emotionally and spiritually. Practice in the mirror with your empowering "I am" and "I have" statements and get in touch with that energy. Each time the reframed thought is stated, state it bolder, louder, and annunciate those strength words.

By following these mind-building and reframing practices, you program yourself with positive, strong, and empowering energy, you are programming yourself to live an abundant, prosperous, and most excellent life!

Contact Stephanie at stephanie@prosperitycoachingetc.com

Prosperity Coaching etc.

43 Church Street

Kingston, NH 03848

603 702-3993

Prosperitycoachingetc.com

The Change 2

Yogini

Yogini is a speaker, author, and a Relationship Breakthrough Specialist, who lives in Castle Rock, Colorado.

Having gone through significant life transitions herself, she has become a catalyst for bringing depth and powerful life experience to her work. She is passionate about empowering everyone to show up fully and authentically in their lives, with passion, presence, and power.

She has inspired people to live with greater vibrancy and awareness by facilitating them to access their innate knowing and cultivating greater self-trust. Her story is one of resilience, bravery and courage. She firmly believes that within every transition lies the opportunity to become who you truly are. Her motto is: "Your life, your business and your relationships are all extensions of the most important relationship you have: the one with yourself."

Coming Home

By Yogini

"If you don't know the nature of fear, then you can never be fearless."

- Pema Chodron

This story is not just about dying, but also about my awakening when I dared to attend life and death with intense awareness.

I'll never forget when, in 2010, I was forced to face my deepest fear. Until this point in my life, I always pushed *it* to the back of my mind. I always thought *it* happens to other people - not me. We don't talk about death in our society, nor do we know how to deal with it when we are faced with death. Yet, it is a transition that each and every one of us must face at some point in our lives. The death of a parent is, perhaps, the most difficult transition to navigate because it is so finite. If you lose a spouse through death or divorce, you can find another mate if you choose to do so, but your parents are not replaceable. Your parents are the reason for your coming into being and they were the first archetypes for male and female role models in your life.

I remember it poignantly… it was the month of September in the year 2010, and my mother was on the phone speaking to me long distance. She asked me, "When are you coming home to see us?" I sensed a slight urgency in her voice, though she downplayed it. She had never asked me anything like this before and I felt a knot in the pit of my stomach. In fact, my mother had never asked very much of me for most of my life. I knew then that it was my time to heed her call, as time does not wait for any one of us. I had not seen my biological family for about six years due to difficult circumstances that didn't allow me the time to go to see them. My life transitions for the past two years required me to be present with my family. My time to return home was long overdue.

Before all this happened, I simply couldn't imagine living without my father being physically present in my life. Two years prior, my father had gotten seriously injured when he slipped and fell. Within months, he was unable to walk and became bedridden. This was a very tall order for a proud man.

In October 2010, I set out to England to see him. You see, I was my daddy's girl. I was the youngest of my siblings and the only daughter in my family. I knew that I was going home to say goodbye to my dearest father. I knew that he had been waiting to see me. It was a deep knowing in my gut.

Whether you're ready or not, sooner or later, the bell tolls. My call came to me in meditation, "You must go to see your father now! He is waiting for you. It's time. His work is done. You must help him to let go. Only you can do this."

I didn't know how I was going to handle this. I easily could have made this situation all about me. How I needed my father to stay alive no matter what… how I didn't want to let go and that I wasn't ready to do so. Deep down, I also knew that he had been suffering silently and was waiting for me. He was waiting to see me so that he could make his final exit.

Although it wasn't easy, I got all my drama and emotions out of the way prior to my departure. I was in emotional turmoil. I was terrified. I felt ill prepared to deal with the monumental task at hand. I was in unknown territory. I felt lost and overwhelmed as I navigated the terrain of facing my father's imminent death. I don't know where I got the courage from, but I dared to meet my fear and rage that was welling up within me.

I had no recourse. I fell to my knees and cried out to God: "Please help me! I don't know how to do this. Help me not to make this about me. Please give me the courage to help him let go!" I started focusing on him in meditation and began projecting loving thoughts to him, "You have been a great father. I am proud of you and honored to be your daughter. Thank you for being such a great teacher in my life! You have played your part exceptionally. Please forgive me if I did anything knowingly or unknowingly to hurt you. I fully forgive you for anything you may have done knowingly and unknowingly to hurt me. It's safe now and time for you to let go. I will be alright. I will make sure that everyone else will be alright as well."

This became my daily mantra that I repeated frequently during the few weeks prior to going home and it helped me maintain some semblance of sanity. I allowed myself to feel all my raw and intense feelings of discomfort, dread, and overwhelming fear. It was the only thing I knew to do at that time. It was only when life forced me to deal with the impending death of my father that I stopped running away and began to fully face my excruciating emotions. I had no choice, but to let go and let God lead the way. I was learning to let go as never before…

surrender was the only way. My one and only priority was to be a pillar of strength for my father in his final days.

My flight seemed never-ending. I was both impatient and desperate to see my father alive because I knew that his days on earth were numbered. Finally, I was home. When I had last seen him he was walking tall and strong. No words can describe how I felt when I came face to face with him for the first time since his accident, and my eyes met with his eyes. His frail body with a tiny face greeted me and I could see the instant joy and relief he felt. At last, his one and only daughter had come home.

It was heartrending to see him so fragile and yet, his eyes were so alive with vibrancy. All my masks slid off as I faced his vulnerability. This was no time to play games. Our roles had shifted. Now, I was the adult and he was the child.

The first four weeks he was radiantly happy to see me. Everyone noticed that his face was glowing. Then, on my birthday, he surprised me by single-handedly shaving his face (something he hadn't done in a long time). Afterwards he asked me, "How do I look?" His face was beaming when I answered, "Super handsome!" It was a priceless memory that I cherish and hold close to my heart.

Each day I was with him, he would ask me to cook him something different and I was happy to do whatever he asked. Prior to my arrival, he had hardly been eating and so I was at his beck and call. I was on a mission: to fulfill my dying father's wishes.

Our bond become such that we spoke without speaking. My father was never a man of many words, but in his final days, he had become even more silent. He would periodically ask me to sit by him and mostly we sat in silence. I would quietly pray and send him healing thoughts about what a great father he was and how grateful I was to be his daughter. I would ask God to surround and comfort him to help ease his suffering. I wanted him to feel safe enough to let go. I think the prayers were more for my sake than his. I felt so utterly helpless.

Once again, all I could do was surrender myself to the situation and realize how futile it was to try to control anything. The cold hard fact was that there was absolutely nothing I could do. It was only when I was faced with this intense life transition that, "being in the present moment" stopped being a mere concept for me. My time had come to practice being fully present with my father.

All my boundaries were melting as I embraced a new found state of increased awareness and deep gratitude for these final bittersweet moments. I cherished every precious moment we had together. I knew that I was being gifted with sacred moments and I had to make them last as long as I could.

He asked me to make him some lentil soup. He insisted that I make it and nobody else. Like a child he asked me in a worried voice, "What if I can only eat one spoonful?" I assured him that he can eat as much or as little as he wanted. Then he hesitated for a moment and asked me in his little boy voice, "Will you feed me today?" This was something he had never asked anyone else to do before because he was always so proud.

Finally, he let me in! He trusted me enough to let me see a side of him that I don't think anyone else had ever seen. I knew that this was not an easy thing for him to do. The acknowledgement and trust I had yearned for all my life was actualized in this moment. He had let down his guard and allowed himself to be defenseless when he asked me to feed him. That was his last meal at home and I knew it because my intuition was heightened.

The next day he told me that he was feeling unwell. Again, he asked me to sit next to him. I knew what he was really telling me: he was tired now and beginning to let go. I told my family this, but they didn't want to face the truth. They all said that he had been close to death so many times before and he would come back, but I knew that this was it. He had indeed overcome death many times before, but this time he was not going to make a comeback. We phoned his relatives and asked them to come and see him. I could feel that his heart was full… his desires were fulfilled. He had seen and met with everyone to the extent he could. His physical condition, by now, had weakened significantly.

Two days later, he had an intensely painful night. His body had become burdened with infection. He readily agreed to go to the hospital, which was something he had never done before willingly. By now, he had also stopped drinking fluids and eating. He had also stopped talking so we could no longer converse with him. In the hospital, it was utterly heartbreaking to hear him in agonizing pain as they tended to his care. While he was in the hospital, my return flight date was getting nearer and nearer. I was booked to come home on Thanksgiving Day and I struggled with making the decision to extend my stay or come back.

My husband and I discussed it and we both concluded that I should go back home to America. We both felt that my Dad's spirit wouldn't depart if I was still there and I wanted his passing to be as painless as possible. I felt as though my heart was stabbed with a thousand knives and the pain seemed like it would never stop. I didn't want to say goodbye so I started making excuses like, "He can't hear me." I don't know if his inability to speak made things better or worse for me, as I too, struggled to find my voice. I knew of course, that deep down his Soul was listening. My husband encouraged me to look into his eyes fully and tell him in his ear everything I wanted to say and, especially, to tell him that I was leaving now and going back to America. Even though it appeared that he couldn't hear me, I know that his Soul heard me.

I held his face in my hands and looked him straight in his eyes. I told him that I loved him very much. I told him how blessed I was to be his daughter. I assured him that he was a great father. I thanked him for being my greatest teacher. Lastly, I told him that he was safe and his work was done. Although he was unable to dialogue with me, his soft eyes and slight smile connected with me and silently signaled to me that he had heard me. Some situations seem insurmountable. What I know for sure is that there is an inner reserve of strength within everyone that can be drawn upon to overcome life's challenges. As I reflect back, I am reminded of Mother Teresa's quote, "God only gives you what you can handle. I just wish he didn't trust me so much."

This was the hardest and most gut wrenching thing I have ever gone through so far in my life. I had stared death in the face. God only knows where I found the nerve to leave and get on the plane. I would never again see my dear father alive again and this realization shattered me. I felt like a thousand shards of glass were piercing into my heart, brutally forcing it to stay open despite my overpowering need to slam it shut so I wouldn't feel the overwhelming grief. I boarded my plane on Thanksgiving Day in great turmoil, devastated to my core, and feeling very much like an orphan. This ultimate sense of abandonment was unlike anything I can begin to describe.

With a broken heart, I returned home on Thanksgiving Day. Four days later my father passed away. I knew the exact moment when it occurred because I physically sensed him leaving my heart. I was driving at the time and I had to pull over because I could feel my body shaking as I started to sob uncontrollably. I tasted the salty sting of death as the waterfall of tears avalanched down my face in full force.

My brother from England called me, but I already knew that my father had crossed over. What I know for sure is that he was loved and that he deeply loved us as well. He did the best for us and loved us to the best of his ability.

I was pushed past the point of breaking which caused a deep transformation within me. I was no longer the person I used to be. I had grown-up and I had learned to be fully present. I learned to trust in a power that was greater than me. I learned to ask, listen, and then follow through on the guidance I received. I was authentic and vulnerable, yet more resilient. My masks slid off. My armor disintegrated. I was fragile, pierced and broken open by devastating loss. I felt the places that were broken inside, yet I also felt the powerful presence of God supporting me. Ever so slowly, the broken places within me began to fill up with light and love. In the midst of my father's passing, I had found grace.

As I watched my father struggle for every last breath, it awakened in me the realization that I was living an unfulfilling life. Grief and loss had opened up a deeper entryway into myself as I struggled to find peace amidst a myriad of chaotic emotions. My own journey towards living full spectrum had just begun.

Our greatest power as human beings is our power to choose. I didn't know that for the longest time until I became real with myself and I used the power of choice. Today, I remind you that you too have a choice.

My message to everyone is that no matter what kind of relationship you have with your parents, please make a conscious effort to make the most of it. If the relationship is difficult, try to make every attempt to heal it. You only get one set of parents and they are irreplaceable. Look beyond the surface issues. Look for the opportunity to learn and grow within the difficulties. Within every challenge lies the opportunity for you to become who you truly are.

Don't wait for death to stare you in the face before you wake up like I did. Don't die with your music still inside of you. My father inspired me to live every day as though it was my last, but it took a harrowing experience for me to realize it.

There is a hospice nurse by the name of Bronnie Ware, who researched the top five regrets of the dying. Do you know what the number one reason was? They wished that they had lived a life being true to themselves instead of fulfilling others' expectations of them.

Your life is precious. How you show up matters.

In the end only three things matter:

Did you live your life fully?

Did you love those that matter?

Did they feel your love?

> "I've learned that people will forget what you said, people will forget what you did, but people will never forget how you made them feel." - Maya Angelou

To contact Yogini:

www.PowerOfShowingUp.com

www.PowerOfShowingUpAuthentically.com

Email Address: yogini@powerofshowingup.com

Stacey Cargnelutti

As an International Best Selling Author of the book series *Living Without Limitations*, a Life, Faith & Fitness Coach, and Creator of 'P3 The Perfect Workout,' Stacey shares her passion for inspired, fit living, worldwide. She educates, inspires and empowers. Her ways provoke thought and help many make the transition from rough, stormy seas, to beautiful, calm sandy beaches. Her desire is to help you experience greater levels of grace and glory as you live out your destined purpose with passion.

Stacey is a seasoned, group exercise veteran with over 35 years experience in the trenches of the fitness industry. She has designed and implemented award winning fitness programs and worked with every age while touching all with her positive, contagious energy, and spirit led life.

Her belief that 'meaningful connection is the key to lasting change and sustained motivation' is authentic, and lived out in all she does. Stacey puts the heart and soul back into fitness and is an inspiration to life itself!

She's a true Agent of Change. Her work empowers all to live higher, go deeper and reach beyond... She uses a blend of word therapy, inspired action, and lots of love to confront complacency and help you reclaim your life and future.

Stacey's heart for people, as well as her passion, enthusiasm, and wisdom, testify of the great wealth of true and total health. May her work inspire you to a prosperous life of divine intimacy, action and impact!

From Faith to Fitness

By Stacey Cargnelutti

"Eat clean and exercise." It sounds easy enough. Ya? Why then the rising epidemic of obesity, the ramped body shame, and the increase in lifestyle-related disease?

Although training methods are 'backed by research,' and people are losing millions of pounds around the globe, few stories end in the lasting change hoped for. The truth is, body transformation as any transformation, comes by faith. Apart from a relevant, meaningful, divine connection, mankind's fuel tank runs dry.

Fitness is nothing more than a state of preparedness that equips one to be ready in season and out, to go, do, and be, without hindrance or limitation. To be fit is to function according to divine design and sustain homeostasis at higher and higher levels of output and intensity. When the spirit, soul, and body align… peace guides, love compels, joy strengthens and fitness flows.

Harmony is a 'congruent arrangement of parts,' the working out of truth. It is real and powerful because it flows only from enlightenment that produces integrity and sincerity. It's the evidence of an authentic connection to personal values, deep seeded convictions and God

Himself. Harmony is spiritual in nature and plays a vital role in the development and maintenance of overall fitness.

Although few argue that faith is the path to ruling and reigning in life, faith-based programming is rarely given a serious platform due to its spiritual and immeasurable nature.

"Faith is the substance of things hoped for and the evidence of things unseen." (Hebrews 11:1)

A measure of faith is given to all. This invisible substance is the divine agent for change and the evidence that you already have what you're hoping for. Faith is energy! It is alive and active and confirmed by corresponding action. When you take a risk and receive the 'anointed utterance' or inspired word and make the choice to believe in what you cannot yet see, your spirit jumps for joy at helping you unleash yourself, live in love, and soar!

The following faith-based programming keys are based on the premise that you are created in the image and likeness of God. You are a speaking spirit, you live in a body, and you have a soul that houses your mind, will, and emotions.

1. Who you are determines what you do.

Defining and connecting with your true identity is always the first step in making positive change. Athletes train, champions win, writers write, and those believing they are healed and victorious align their lives with health and victory. So before we go any further, 'Who do you say you are?' Close your eyes for a moment and imagine you at your very best. How do you look, feel, think, speak, decide, act, and move? This is the real you.

In seeing yourself strong, determined, well-able, and fully equipped, you begin to take on this identity in thought, word and deed. Soon you are manifesting the true you. And when you are ready to see more and get even greater results, you will open up your spiritual eyes and embrace more of the greatness seeded within.

"It is no longer I who live but Christ who lives in me…" Galatians 2:20

Contained in this one revelation is unlimited power and potential, and tremendous intrinsic motivation! When you believe that you are, you will be, and therefore do.

2. Real and lasting change is spiritual and happens in the context of relationship.

Did you know that your drive for connection is greater than your drive for food? You are a relational being. "It is not good that mankind be alone…" God said, "I will make him a helper suitable." I believe social media has given us some pretty good evidence regarding our need for connection even in the shallows of life, but when it comes to making lasting change, deep, meaningful connection with God and others is vital. This is why God calls us to Himself and not to morality, mental ascension or religious ritual. Spiritual consciousness, godly character, and personal power are the evidence of divine connection and not the means to acquiring it.

Because you are a triune being created in the image and likeness of God, your body, soul (mind, will, emotions), and spirit fail to function optimally independent of one another. Disorder, misalignment and disconnect radically effect performance and function. Can you imagine the chaos that reigns when your spirit nods off and neglects its role of leadership? Of course the body and soul are ready and willing to 'step up,' but neither is designed to lead and therefore they lack the equipping and grace to be effective.

The body and soul are responders. They make decisions based on past experience, safety and comfort, vs. wisdom and integrity. Their leadership results in powerless sensuality and egocentric narcissism. Beware!

Your awakened spirit holds the power to give you the body of your dreams and all other desires of your heart. According to divine design, the chain of command is as follows: Spirit. Soul. Body. Your body is subject to you, not you to it. Allowing it to usurp will disqualify you from the race and life is not a spectator sport! You are in it to win it!

Man's spirit is called the 'lamp of the Lord' because it holds the thoughts, feelings and intentions of God's heart and illuminates paths of righteousness so you can know and enjoy life to the full. Spirit-led living is the path to honor, power and glory.

God's deep desire is YOU. And secondly, that you experience the power of divine intimacy. The unforced rhythms of grace that flow from the heart of God through the conduit of meaningful and divine romance are for the purpose of ushering mankind into the power and glory he is designed to know and in so knowing, bring heaven to earth.

Love compels, restrains, expresses itself and changes all it touches - including your body. Transformation flows freely in love and becomes purposeful in fulfilling the plan of God for your life. Sustaining love is to sustain MOJO! Knowing that you are from love, sustained by love, and purposed for love, is the realization that empowers you to conquer all. You are a force to be reckoned with, but if you don't 'deep down know it,' you will lack confidence, direction and motivation.

Disconnecting any area of your life from your essence of love is to unplug from your fuel source, lose power, and 'die.' Burnout happens to those living in the realm of the natural. Attempting body transformation apart from a spirit to Spirit connection is to 'run the car on three cylinders instead of four' and forfeit great power.

3. All you need is desire and oxygen.

God's words are the truest expression of the real you. They reveal your deepest needs and unveil your deepest desires. "Delight yourself in the Lord and He'll give you the desires of your heart." (Psalm 37:4) Your desire is a prophetic picture of God's perfect will for your life. Few are skilled at identifying their desires because they mistake desire for controlling lust and identify with their sinful, sensual nature more than their redeemed, true and divine nature. It takes the brutal honesty, supreme wisdom, and supernatural power of intimacy with God, to align your intentions with your actions.

We fight and quarrel because our passions and desires war within us; we don't have what we want. And although we may ask, we ask for the wrong things.

The blueprint for your best body is in your spirit. Your life as well as your body, is hidden with Christ in God, which means He is the way to attaining health, strength and weight loss. All these things are worked out of you by grace through faith in the realm of the spirit as you renew your mind and abide in truth.

When desire has its rightful way, your life and the 'blueprint' match. This place of harmony aligns you with the abundant life you are designed and destined for. It's a place of no compromise, complacency, or burnout because none of these exist in the spirit. To live in alignment with your true self is to know the wealth of health as well as the power to sustain it. Once you taste the bliss and high energy of connecting with your source of inspiration and living out your intentions, all else pales and your tolerance for compromise will cease.

To ignite the 'fire of desire' needed to fuel your change, ask yourself, "Who am I and what do I look, feel, and move like?"

What does a fit body give you? How does this fit body fulfill your deepest needs of certainty, variety, significance, connection, contribution, growth, and creativity?

Your reasons for doing the work of body transformation need to be compelling! They need to inspire and move you into action and produce results that last. Hiring a 'pusher' will buy you some time, but sooner or later it comes back to you and your desire for change.

Relevant, living faith is the oxygen that fuels your desire and inspires you to take action toward it. Reading the inspired words, listening to stories of transformation, observing lifestyles you can appreciate, developing character, and doing what you respect others for doing, are a few ways to stay aligned with your God-given desires.

It's the fire that burns off the dross, lightens the load, illuminates the path, and moves you in heart-centered ways. Desire is a powerful grace intended to move you onward and upward in good and godly directions of love, life, health, peace, power and joy and bring you into perfect harmonic flow: spirit, soul, body.

4. Nothing happens until something moves.

Because the words of God are alive and active, they work in you 'both to will and to do.' And because they are spirit, they quicken your physical body and move you into action. Your spirit has been appointed the job of leadership and when it's given authority, it empowers you in transcending human expectation! The more time you spend in the word of God the more harmony and resurrection power you will operate in and know.

Just as your natural body was formed from the dust of the ground and requires natural substance to sustain life and growth, so your spirit was formed of Spirit and requires spiritual food to sustain life and growth. The words of God are spirit, truth and life. They set you free to show up in full power and presence and reclaim your life.

Not only is faith your true fuel supply but it's also the mirror that reveals the real you. You are not to wait for heaven to enjoy the freedom and power of abundant life, your inheritance of authority, health, hope, wholeness, light, wisdom, love… is for now. Your mission and mandate is to bring heaven to earth.

As the incorruptible, spiritual seed of the word manifests, the person, life, and power of Christ is revealed to and through you. When He appears, the sobering realization that you are 'like Him' begins to have its life-changing way in your heart and you become unstoppable! Soon, the glory given you begins to touch the world in naturally, supernatural ways. (1 John 3:2, John 17:22)

As I mentioned earlier, your physical body is subject to you according to divine order. Keep it under you! One of the biggest mistakes we make is giving authority to the body and soul by subjecting ourselves to inferior mindsets that lead us to the pantry and couch rather than the juice bar or gym. Exercise produces profit because it requires you to do the hard thing by sowing to the spirit and growing the inner man rather than giving preference to comfort and ease, sowing to the flesh, and reaping destruction.

Every new move of God begins with a new sound. Worshipers led troops into battle, walls fell down with a shout, and no one crosses a finish line alone. Victory has a voice! This may sound a bit weird but your throat is really a birth canal for 'spiritual babies.' Meaning, nothing happens that hasn't first been spoken.

A friend of mine described the wall she hit at mile twelve of a half marathon she was running. As fatigue set in, a voice from the sideline shouted, "Go Laura! You got this!!!" It was the word she needed to inspire her last mile and finish her race.

Both life and death are in the power of the tongue, angels move to accomplish the will of God when they hear a voice of truth, and demons move to execute evil when they hear perversity (words contrary to the will of God). Your words move heaven and hell and attach meaning and emotion (energy in motion) to everything. They are the literal substance creating peace, bringing joy, building bodies, strengthening relationships or destroying everything; you decide. Your tongue unleashes great power in your life and on the earth.

As the leader of your life, can you detect areas of misalignment? Speak order over the chaos. Just as God saw darkness and said, "Let there be light," you are designed to 'call those things that are not as though they are.' Call your body "healthy, strong, slim, fit, and able..." There is grace in the spoken word that longs to work on your behalf. In Genesis 1, we find God's 'formula' for creation... "God said..., and it was so." When you believe that what you say is coming your way, your thoughts, feelings, words and ways will begin to align with your desires and manifest abundant life. God spoke and 'it was,' time and again, because nothing within Him resisted. His whole being was in harmony and not at war within itself.

In what areas are you living contrary to your intentions or desires? In what ways do you resist love and life?

You are not in your situation to experience it, you are there to change it with faith working through love. See the reality of your situation and speak life, love, divine order and health over it. Stir up your desire for more! Then be the architect of your life and create the body and the reality you are here to know… by faith.

5. Train your senses to discern good.

"Taste and see that the Lord is good!" (Psalm 34:8)

Why? Because your body remembers only what it feels or senses, in order to keep your motivation high, positive associations with desired behaviors need to be made.

Every behavior is motivated by the result it produces. According to hedonic theory, you will approach what helps and avoid what hurts. We are all self-regulated by a variety of motives, but understanding that pain and pleasure are baselines can bring clarity on cloudy days and get you to the gym when you'd prefer other options.

Choosing life and profit over death and defeat is not natural for most, and therefore requires grace to achieve. Not only do you need grace to take action, you need grace to discern your life support team. Right now, in your midst, are resources and people ready to help you achieve your goals. Train your spiritual eyes to recognize them. You will find at least one person, place, or thing equipped and ready to move you in right directions daily, if you are sincerely looking. None of us cross finish lines alone.

Just like the word of God, your desire carries the needed grace to make change. Whether you're training a dog to obedience, a child to wisdom, or an adult to healthy, inspired living, the pleasure pain principle applies. New associations to pleasure are established by disciplining yourself to the new behavior until momentum kicks in and a new kind of pleasure is experienced and associated with the behavior. Before you know it, the old ways become painful and easy to resist. I say resist because there will always be a pull toward living in the flesh, but it loses its power as you exercise authority over it daily.

Change happens when the pain of being a caterpillar outweighs the pain of becoming a butterfly. When you're sick and tired of being sick and tired, 'BAM!' the grace to change arrives.

It's important to see resistance as a thief trying to break in to the house of God (you, His temple), and steal life, love and hope from you. Until you're courageous enough to arise and shine as YOU, he'll find a way in. And until you're willing to give up relationships that are not serving the life and destiny in you, he'll find a way in.

What are the foods, habits, people and places that need to be left behind in order for you to take hold of new and better things? The body you want is yours. It's waiting to be 'claimed.' You will prove your desire for it by acting accordingly in these three areas:

a. Authority. Your ability to keep the thief out of your way and maintain divine order and therefore, proper function continually.

b. Discipline. Your diligence in establishing healthful rituals to keep you on course and running to win.

c. Love. Your ability to express a sincere desire for life, blessing and the perfect will of God.

Closing To Do List:

• Connect daily with compelling reasons you are pursuing change in your body.

• See your new body with your spiritual eyes or imagination.

- Feel the emotions you have in this new body.

- Explore the new tastes, smells and orientations of living in this new body.

- Think and speak in the affirmative concerning your body, "I am healed, strong, well-able, diligent, energized…"

- Through practice, train your thoughts to righteousness, senses to wisdom, and body to health.

To Contact Stacy:

Stacey Cargnelutti ~ Amore Vita Coaching and Consulting

StaceyC.com ~ Higher Ways & Better Things

Contact me: stacey@staceyc.com

Connect with me: www.facebook.com/StaceyC.com

The Change 2

Darcey Pollard

Darcey Pollard is a peak performance strategist based in Melbourne, Australia, who has helped clients internationally achieve new levels of success in both their personal and professional lives. For the last four years, he has primarily worked with businesses to improve team productivity, communication and leadership skills. By improving teams, he assists his clients in achieving higher client retention, greater revenue and growth. Darcey has consulted with some of Australia's largest retailers, been published in collaborative works twice previous and has also been ranked as a *Top 100 Professional Coach* by LifeCoachHub. A person who holds high expectations from both himself and his clients, Darcey is constantly seeking those that are "doing it better" so that he can then learn their principles to success and put these into a system everybody can use. Outside of the professional arena, Darcey is passionate about self-improvement and championing others to lead their ideal lives and can often be found enjoying the company of others or with his head in a quality book.

Achieving Connection Through Disconnecting

By Darcey Pollard

Despite being the most connected society in the history of the human race, research shows that we may also be the loneliest. A study in the United Kingdom found that 1 in 10 Britons consider themselves lonely. In Canada, nearly 25% of people consider themselves lonely, while research in Australia found that 27% of Australians aged 25 - 44 frequently referred to themselves in the same way. Additionally, two studies in the United States found that 40% of people report that they're lonely. When we combine these conclusions with the findings of a report that was published in *Science*, things become a little more urgent. In 1987, researchers found that social isolation "is as significant to mortality rates as smoking, high blood pressure, high cholesterol, obesity and lack of physical exercise." In his book *Emotional Intelligence*, Daniel Goleman expands on these findings with further research that declares, "smoking increases mortality risk by a factor of just 1.6, while social isolation does so by a factor of 2.0, making it a greater health risk." Who would have thought that being socially isolated can increase your chance of death?

In this chapter we are going to look at overcoming social isolation and loneliness in the 21st century. What causes loneliness when our society is so connected? Could our constant 'always on' connection be the cause of our perceived loneliness? Are our interactions with each other online creating less than complete relationships? Are these relationships just illusions?

Before we dive into that, it is important to better understand loneliness and the factors that contribute to its presence. Loneliness is defined by the Oxford Dictionary as 'sadness because one has no friends or company.' Using this definition we are able to extract the likely factors relating to one experiencing this emotion; an absence of happiness, the lack of approval, inclusion or sense of belonging from others, a lack of physical interaction, higher levels of anxiety, a fewer number of fulfilling relationships, and negative self-talk such as "nobody likes me," "I don't have anybody that supports/loves me," "I wish I had their life," or "why doesn't anyone want to hang out with me?" These factors may also lead to low self-worth which in turn may lead the individual to shy away from the world, exacerbating the problem. A person can have many social contacts and still feel lonely.

This widening experience of loneliness seems to be reported today in greater numbers than in any previous years. So what's changed? It seems that the more connected we are with the outside world, the more we are isolating and emotionally disengaging from each other. The relationships that are being forged today online via email, text messaging, and social media seem to be void of the substance that flows within relationships we form when we are together in the same room. And even then, everybody has a focus that is directed elsewhere - to some kind of mobile device. It is a rare occasion when people in the same room are totally present for one another.

Part 1 – The 21st Century Enabler of Loneliness

On one hand, there are doubtlessly advantages to digital communication - from being able to instantly communicate and share content, to making new connections with people globally. The effects of digital communication are still being researched and may not be the direct cause for the increase in rates of loneliness worldwide. Nevertheless, these new forms of communication *are* having some impact. Two areas that are found to have an impact on both our lives and our relationships are social media and mobility devices.

Facebook has been found to enhance one's level of social capital. This is positively connected to psychological well-being and happiness for people with low self-esteem. Social media also allows us to selectively present the best version of ourselves to the world, which has also been found to increase self-esteem. It is at this point that we enter murky waters.

The idea of selectively presenting your life lends to the illusion of an 'idealized' life, that is to say, the only reason that selectively presenting one's life on social media raises self-esteem is because individuals have a tendency to make it look as though they live a perfect life. This feeds the possibility that we are too concerned with how others are perceiving us. When we are viewing the profiles of other people who are showing their 'perfect lives,' we may experience feelings of inferiority which may have a negative effect on self-esteem.

Teens are most likely to be affected by this, as not only are they the majority of consumers of this type of information, they are also at the age of development that has a lot to do with social interaction and acceptance from peer groups. Behavior that occurs during this period may continue into their adult years as they find the most appropriate ways to handle particular situations. For some teens, social media plays a bigger role than others. And for a lot of teens, the reaction to their photos and posts on social media has a direct effect on their feelings. A survey of 1000 people by meQuilibrium found that 61% of people felt jealous, depressed, and sad or annoyed after reading posts on social media. People tend to be naturally concerned with the opinions of others. After all, this relates closely to fitting in, which is an important asset for survival.

Approval from others may have a direct impact on our self-esteem. For most people, approval means belonging, and belonging is a basic need. So, for many people, approval becomes a significant motivator, and other people's opinions may guide their decisions. While sometimes this can be beneficial or helpful, many times it also becomes an obstacle or a factor that has too much weight on one's decisions and self-esteem. The centrality of approval to people's decisions is likely to have originated a long time ago, in times where people lived in small, isolated groups where exile was equivalent to death, since a person outside of the community would not be able to survive. Disapproval could have very serious consequences, such as being unable to find a partner among the community, or conduct trade for different objects necessary for survival. However, in the current society, people have a much wider pool of options for interaction.

People are conditioned to care from childhood. The opinions of parents and teachers play a big role in education and learning, such as understanding the difference between right and wrong. Recognition is a reinforcement for certain types of behaviors, while disapproval works as a deterrent for other types. Parents' opinions shape a child's idea of self-worth, eventually also having a lot to do with how this child will perceive himself or herself, as well as how much weight other people's opinions will have on the person later in life.

In that respect, social media, for some people, becomes a platform of expression that is mediated by selective self-presentation. People are always connected to people who evaluate their presentation, so the person has a conscience of an audience that may be real in some aspects, and not so real in others. People evaluate the content they want to upload in terms of how other people will evaluate it.

Some people are more influenced by others' opinions, others are not. However, it's safe to say that for most people, the opinion of others is an important factor. People who are most swayed by other's opinions are those who experience a stronger activation of the brain reward centre when others agree or validate their own ideas. The feeling of reward when others agree can be connected with wide spreading trends or importance of communication through social media - a "like" can signify approval and thus activate the rewards circuits in the brain. So most people use social media to post things that will get them "interactions" that activate the reward centre and make themselves feel good. It does not move us to a space of connectedness with another person, it is simply an empty interaction. When 50 people "like" something, can you recall who liked it? Do you then thank them or somehow interact further?

It was found that people were almost three times more likely to express their opinions if they thought their audience or their followers agreed with them. Often, people also feel more reluctant to discuss their opinions through social media if they think that not all of their followers agree with their opinions on controversial issues.

It would seem that social media is becoming less about building relationships, but more so to boost our ego. This is where loneliness comes to play because the very actions that we believe are making us feel included and valued are serving only the person who posted the material. Our posts do not act to serve and enhance the relationship between two people. Social media should be utilized this way, however this tends not to be the case.

As we shift away from social media to another form of digital communication we can see the effects continue. Smartphones are arguably the most common platform for digital communication. They allow us to communicate via text, voice, video, and images and most importantly, remain connected *all of the time*. With a constant connection to the outside world, this give us the great advantage of being autonomous and flexible in where and how we work. Like selective presentation on social media, smartphones and their level of connectedness are a double edge sword.

Some research suggests that being connected 24/7 may have a negative impact on happiness. The clearest demonstration of this are employees who cannot define the boundary between work and personal life. This may occur because they are constantly available, checking emails or taking calls away from the office. This constant connection can lead to an increase in stress, anxiety and lowered happiness.

With a constant connection, digital communication can become a ceaseless tool to attack and undermine a person's self-esteem and wellbeing. The constant connection to our smart phones and other forms of communication may be enabling the rise of cyber bullying and harassment in both teens and adults. This form of bullying varies from traditional bullying in that it can be continued constantly, even when the person is away from the bullies. It can use offensive videos, messages, images and so on, that can be distributed anonymously, instantly, and to a large amount of people. The harassing content cannot be easily deleted. As there is little escape for a victim of cyber bullying, this may lead to feelings of anxiety, and forced isolation in an attempt to avoid the hurt.

There is strong evidence that shows being connected 24/7 may be harmful. The effects of being constantly engaged with social media and technology may lead to feelings of inferiority, jealousy, depression, sadness, anger, anxiety, and forced isolation. All of which can emerge as we are looking for ways to gain immediate gratification through social interaction that we think is crafting a connection of approval and belonging, rather than adding true value to our relationships. We are focusing on what is in it for us. When we are online we aren't building relationships, we are disengaging from those physically around us while we mistakenly attempt to boost our self-worth.

Part 2 – Remedies To The Digital Age

Given all that has been discussed, there is evidence that how we communicate has a profound impact on our relationships and how we perceive ourselves. There are clearly benefits to being a part of our digital age, as well as emerging damaging effects when we linger in this type of world for too long.

For the present day being, how do we cope? How do we minimize the damages that may arise from too much exposure to this world? And what about our future generations where digital communication has become more deeply integrated; how can we manage ourselves so as to maintain fulfilling relationships?

Firstly, we must learn to disconnect. A big reason that we are facing these problems is simply because we are choosing to give ourselves no down time. From work to home and from home to work there is an almost 100% 'uptime.' There are some people, a few you may know, whose only time they are offline is when they are sleeping.

Going 'off the grid' has been shown to increase productivity, the ability to solve problems, enhance emotional management, and improve sleep quality. To put this into action, start small and arrange for half an hour of complete downtime. Slowly work your way up, eventually getting yourself to one day a week. Disconnecting from the world not only teaches you that the world won't fall apart when you take a break from it, but it also lends to this second point - enjoying your own company.

Many people choose to stay connected so often because it gives them a false sense of belonging to be connected virtually with others, and avoids them being left in the room, alone, with themselves. Today, most people know other people better than they know themselves, and to sustain a healthy relationship, this needs to be the other way around.

If you are someone who may sometimes experience bouts of loneliness (which I believe almost every one of us does at some point), just notice where you focus your time. Is it on yourself and your personal development, or is it on others and how they might perceive you? Now this is not to say that caring about others or their opinions is bad or detrimental, only that when you solely exist to impress others and are disregarding your own needs does it become a problem, and you may need to re-assess. When we believe that to belong, we need everybody to like us, and that disagreeing or having a different point of view is to somehow not belong, our wellbeing as an individual is marginalized.

We begin to devalue ourselves, we lose our own voice. Our beliefs and values are perceived as no longer important, who we are and what we stand for are overshadowed, and the plethora of negative effects that we have explored in this chapter all creep in like monsters in the dark. To keep our sense of individuality we need to do two things. Firstly, grow as an individual, pick up a self-development book - as you're doing right now - or audio program and learn about you, the gallery of emotions you feel, and your mindset; become your own master. Secondly, build a strong support group with real people. Humans require physical interaction with each other to exist and feel connected. No digital connection can foster the same feeling of connectedness and belonging that can be achieved when we spend time sitting face to face with someone.

Earlier it was mentioned that digital relationships are void of substance. What is meant by substance? Presence is the first constituent that is missing. To be present for another you are fully in the moment with those around you. Maybe you are at dinner with friends and all conversing about the golf trip you were on last month, watching the big screen enthralled at the movies, or lying on the grass star gazing embracing the silence. Presence is an ethereal connection that doesn't require words or sight, it is felt and relies on being close to another, enjoying the same activity. When someone is on their phone, distracted, you can feel the attention is missing, that they are occupied elsewhere.

Another element of this substance is empathy, or the ability for a person to identify and share the emotions of another. Typically empathy is learned and enriched by understanding body language and facial expressions and how these relate to certain emotions and states. Speaking to someone via text and having the same conversation face to face yield varying empathic responses (or lack of).

When we limit the number of hours we spend connected online, and increase the number of hours spent face to face with others, our perspectives begin to change, our outlook on life brightens, and one becomes fulfilled more easily and tends to be more comfortable taking risks in life. There comes a certain feeling of safety when you have strong friendships that serve as your foundation to life.

Finally, to turn around loneliness and isolation, stop comparing to others. Each person is experiencing their own journey through life and, as such, cannot be compared to another. Comparing two lives is to compare an apple to a car. Instead of competing with Mr. Jones, compete with yourself, become better than yesterday. Set yourself bigger goals, and strive to become the best version of you, it is far too frivolous trying to be better than somebody else.

Social media and technology should be utilized in ways that help us move forward in building better relationships with one another. It is about giving great value to the other person. To really thrive in this age of digital communication we need to recognize that our digital connections are illusory. They do not represent the same things as "real" physical, in person relationships. They can never be replaced, our online presence exists as an addition, it's an extra, another form in which to strengthen existing relationships, but only as long as we are adding value and remembering that we must also be enjoying time with our friends, families and colleagues offline. It is with those people that we get to foster our community and our tribes, here is where we get our support, our sense of belonging, and these are the people that show you that love, joy, happiness, gratitude and sense of self-worth that is found within you. You won't find this connection online. To change your life, simply switch off, disconnect, look away from your phone and engage with the people around you and just notice how your world transforms.

Contact Info:

Email:

darcey.pollard@mrdarceycoaching.com

Website: www.mrdarceycoaching.com

The Change 2

Tamara Renee

Tamara believes that everyone deserves to be "living" ... having active, flowing and thriving lives.

Her passion is to guide her clients to experience each moment of their lives by balancing your body, opening your mind and inspiring your dreams.

Tamara has developed methods that cracks open YOUR code for the ideal diet and life. She has a quarter century experience in transforming people like you into living your healthiest and most confident life.

Your Food-Truth

By Tamara Renee

Envision this... YOU, a caterpillar trudging through the dirt; dodging footsteps and curious passersby. There are hours slipping away as you continue moving forward inch by inch and finally stopping to build a cocoon shielding you from old to new. Saying good bye to the former you as you know it. In order to break free into your newfound world, you will have to work... WORK... your way through the cocoon to emerge as that beautifully stunning butterfly. Your wings are strong and spirit stronger. You exude confidence coupled with grace.

As a human we, too, have many challenges that lead us- hopefully – to our rebirthing and emergence as a stronger, more confident and graceful being. This brings to question...what truly comes first? Is it the dropping of the egg that generates the creation of a caterpillar? Is it the caterpillar's struggle to its cocoon that defines you or is it the freedom from the cocoon that brings out your radiance? What is your dirt... and your struggle to ultimately reaching your health and body goals.

There's no secret that we need food as our fuel. The question would be, is food your crutch, your dirt? Do you struggle to separate emotion from your desire and/or need for food? Do you find yourself hunting to quench your void, your sorrow, with chocolate or wine?

Stop ignoring that your immediate pleasure comes with a heavy price. Brain fog, bloating, weight gain, mood swings are now the catalyst to your anger. You feel disgusted with yourself. In the end, what is your Food-Truth?

Are your food choices created by your emotions? Is broccoli your fuel or your poison? This is not a cookie cutter answer. Just like your dress size, this is not a one fits all solution; but where do you start?

How do you crack your code? Do you go with the local nutritionist? Or the latest fad diet? What is your method? How do you choose? I'm a firm believer that everyone's method is different. In order to find your starting line there must be a foundation, a factual base to build up from. What do each of us have that is always just our own? Attitude and DNA. Let's investigate why and how this benefits Y O U individually rather than a warehoused fad diet.

Can food help you suppress habits and behaviors that may be innate to your DNA? Yes, by regulating your personal systems and blood sugar levels, you may be able to suppress the cravings, snacking gene, satiety gene, yoyo gene, obesity gene, and the metabolic syndrome gene. Your body's constant and precise Reactive Response to food is always with you. You're carrying your Reactive Response Tool everywhere. It's your undeniable truth. The utmost scientific techniques, paired with your intuitive observations will pointedly answer, "How do I, personally, unlock my body's dietary code?"

Know that, without a doubt, food can cause health and confidence levels to plummet. One of my clients who comments on her decision to scientifically investigate her method through DNA states that, "My lack of self-esteem, and overall health and weight have become all consuming. It's taken my quality of life and I have to get it back. I've spent years dodging old friends in the aisles of stores for fear of what they might say - my confidence and self esteem are gone. I've missed so much time from enjoying family events to playing with my kids during some of the most formidable years. Time I can never get back. I have the opportunity to break the cycle here. To scientifically define what is making my body tick and how to oil the clock."

More notably, as described in detail by Chris Bell of the UK newspaper, *The Telegraph*. You actually leave a mark on the genes that you pass down. The old adage that 'you got that from your father' is not too far off. Through epigenome research, it is has been found that your bad habits will modify your genes and be passed down to future generations. There is no "do-over" or fresh start for the generations to come. If you adopt eating or smoking habits that will impede your health and wellness today, then there may very well be change to your structure, a type of scar, to put it simply.

It's time to ask yourself the core question: Why do I cry out for more in life? What is it I'm aching and deeply yearning for in order to feel this life; to live in the here and now? Why am I here but not present?

Even Cinderella had to work for her fairytale. There isn't a magical fix. That being said, there is hope on the horizon. We can talk all day in theories and analogies… floating around like a butterfly, but you cannot transform your experience in life without implementing change. How do you change? Well, you need to get the facts - the nitty gritty. So this is where you jump into the magic bus of learning and information! Begin your Food-Truth journey by assessing and implementing these key factors as they relate to you:

- Directive Diet Plan - Your body's innate Reactive Response Tool

- Nutritional Guidelines - Basic fundamentals that cannot be ignored

- Action - The integration of method meets lifestyle - livable, maintainable, sustainable

You will find progress using these tips, but without YOUR specific recipe... your scientifically factual dietary needs... these are merely guidelines to satiate the craving you have for knowledge TODAY.

The Directive Diet Plan

By definition, the Directive Diet Plan is the body's Reactive Response Tool to food.

Do you find your body speaking to you with any of these specific symptoms?

Dizziness

Poor memory

Foggy thinking

Learning disorders

Seizures

Paranoia

Arthritis

Eczema

Asthma

Headache

Sneezing

Runny or stuffy nose

Puffy, watery or itchy eyes

Blurred vision

Earache

Hearing loss

Sore throat

Itching in the roof of the mouth

Candidiasis

Canker sores

Sinusitis

Aggressive behavior

Coughing

Chest pain

Heart irregularities

Sudden changes in blood pressure

Nausea, vomiting

Diarrhea

Constipation

Abdominal pains or cramps

Rashes

Insomnia

Chronic fatigue

Swelling of the hands or feet

Urinary frequency or urgency

Vaginal itching

Excessive hunger or binge eating

Depression

Hyperactivity (ADD/ADHD)

Emotional instability or hypersensitivity

Panic attacks

Seizures

The Nutritional Guidelines:

It's often thought that man has created a simplified, streamlined, ultimate platform for productivity. Think about it... is processed shredded cheese making your life, your dinner, easier? Can life truly be easier if you're body is processing plastic? How productive can you be if you're body is in a tired, bloated, brain-fogged, overwhelmed, and immune deficient state? The answer is simple. This isn't rocket science. The answer is in the green... not money... broccoli!

Think back to a time of pure, chemical-free produce, meat, and dairy. Your health wasn't better because you were younger. Look at kids today. Back then you ate balanced meals. You actually spent time enjoying exercise with a walk to the movies or a ride through town on a bike. Sure, time moves faster, streets are busier, but that doesn't mean you need to be out of balance. You need to refocus, find the tools to level your body's chemistry out and the rest will fall into place. This is all but required for you to LIVE in the HERE and NOW, happy.

Now put your listening ears (or eyes) on. It is important to STOP and note some of the most basic things that will keep you OFF balance and how to counteract them:

Quality vs Quantity:

It doesn't get any simpler than this: organic foods are always best. Most natural, non-chemical, non-modified, items will taste better and fuel your body more efficiently. Your day will be brighter and there will be more spring in your step as your blood sugar levels stabilize. So before you put the ice cream in your shopping cart, ask yourself, "Is this a healthy choice?"

If you are keeping your food journal, you can review it after a week and circle all of your questionable food choices and aim to correct those the following week. Remember, no one is perfect.

Sleep:

Umm… this is mandatory not optional. Men need at least 7 hours of sleep and women need 8 hours of sleep. Ideally at night. In your bed, not on your couch. Lack of sleep is a silent life-sucker. Really. Think about it. How many times have you forgotten something important and followed it with the ever-common statement, "I'm sorry. I didn't sleep well last night." Perhaps you can fake it there, but what about your attention span. Are there days where your attention span is less than a gnat? Do you wonder why that morning commute is more stressful and the gum chewing in the next cubicle is grating at your last nerve? Does all of this sound depressing… If you answer "yes" then I have to ask you, are you sleeping at night?

Digestive Health:

Do not be fooled. Your digestive system contains 80% of your immune system. It is the gateway to health and happiness.

We live in a culture of addiction for Starbucks, cookies, and a nice glass of Pinot Noir… but in that, where is your Food-Truth? Where does the REAL you lie? Imagine being free from the bloating, brain fog and crankiness. But how? Here are some of the tricks to guide you in your quest for digestive relief:

Stay Hydrated:

You should be drinking enough WATER to be equal to ½ your weight in ounces (100 lbs ÷ 2 = 50 oz). If you drink caffeine (coffee, tea, soda) then keep chuggin' that water my friend, keep chuggin'.

Keep Active:

Help that poop move through your system… get your groove on or walk around the block, ride a bike, jump on a mini-trampoline, (it's not just for kids anymore!) but keep on movin' especially if you have a history of digestive issues.

Dietary Key Points:

We have a variety of factors that seem to conspire, ultimately deteriorating or supporting a degenerated devastation to your system. Solution? Eat fiber. Eat greens - many, many greens. Eat sensibly by eating a variety, and a bit from the rich macronutrient (not mac as in Big Mac) category. Sounds simple enough right? Only your DNA will be able to tell you which fats are affecting your system the most. Until then, you'll have to get back to the rule of quality over quantity. Also, make note of what might be irritating your body using the Reactive

Response Tool that comes with your DNA on the day you are born. It is a ginormous indicator for defining YOUR FOOD-TRUTH.

I'm a big fan of coconut oil. It has joined the super foods categories and has an antimicrobial to fight harmful bacteria and yeast. The upside... yes the upside is that it can make your tummy hurt, that is if you've got bacterial overgrowth. This is because it is killing those buggers. You may want to try to swish it around in your mouth to activate your enzymes, or use it in supplement form for digestion. It has also been known as an appetite suppressant that is heart friendly, yet a fat that can make you thinner. It's also considered to have a stimulatory effect on the metabolism. It's helped neurological conditions and as mentioned, it can counteract the bacteria in the gut.

Olive oil, raw butter, and lamb fat are also notable. Those that have taken a daily dose of 1-2 tablespoons of an organic variety, have sworn by its benefits.

Turmeric is in line for a "Lifetime Achievement Award" as well. Known for its anti-inflammatory and antioxidant properties, it will protect the mitochondria and in step, it will improve glucose metabolism, both of which are fundamentals in the brain game - reducing one's risk for brain disease. You can tame pain with turmeric simply by its own healing qualities. In composition alone, its created with the active ingredient, curcuma. Curcuma lowers the level of the enzymes that cause inflammation. Being a spice, you can use it in its purest form and sprinkle it over your food. Of course, the option is there for it in supplement form as well. Some other worthy positive mentions have been on skin and digestive issues from consistent turmeric use.

It's not a race. You are allowed to CHEW your food. Put your fork down while you are chewing and relax. You don't need to rush through it. It's called dinner-TIME and lunch-TIME because you are taking a break in TIME for dinner or lunch.

True it sounds a little intense. However, it is amazing stuff; it eases symptoms from a cold or the like, while enhancing energy levels. In fact, it's a fantastic support to an antibiotic. Probiotics are the microorganisms usually found in the digestive system where the "positive bacteria" is used to balance out the "negative bacteria." The Tufts-New England Medical Center research team is working on the study of probiotics and its effectiveness on antibiotic-resistant bacteria. This particular study is focusing on the benefit of those with major infections who have lowered immune systems and are in the care of a hospital or nursing home.

The information on probiotics does not stop there. In the book, *Grain Brain* by Dr. Perlmutter, you can explore it in more depth. Specifically, how probiotics positively affect stress, anxiety and depression levels when included in a diet with food that is high in said probiotics.

Weight:

Do we really need to talk about it? Weight. It's a heavy subject. No, seriously, there is one point we want to get out of the way. Is it weight that has you knocking at your Food -Truth's door? Well, c'mon in! Whatever drives you to improving your health… we're in!

To optimize your health, always strive to be your ideal weight.

Stress Management:

Learn to be one with your 'Zen.' If you are always in turmoil and drama then you will have nothing but a rolled up, wrung out, intestinal track. Sound like fun? No? Then I take it you are opting for stress management. Good choice. Let's get it before it gets us! Stress can be as serious as handling an illness or death. Stress can be caused in multiple ways and by multiple things. In fact, just by multi-tasking you can be "stressing out." Either way, studies have shown that too much hardship, challenge or change can cause an increase in the risk of illness. When you're feeling like you are in a state of stress, try to reason with it. First be aware of the heightened emotion. Try to be reasonable about the severity of it. Don't be hesitant to ask for help when needed. Dedicate yourself to getting better sleep and exercising as a strategy. Caffeine is not the helper here... I stress the word NOT. Be sure to limit your intake.

It's always good to try to stay in front of stress. Use good time management and healthy sleep habits. Don't forget to laugh at yourself. Have a sense of humor about it and learn how to modify negative self statements. This means no more slamming on the horn or tailgating people, yelling at the TV, or engaging in water cooler drama... you basically need to create your own 'Zen.' How? You would be amazed at what a balanced diet will do for your self-confidence, body language, mood, and of course, that all rolls right into your stress level. You can consider meditation, yoga, or breathing exercises. All of these are valuable techniques to manage your stress because, honestly, sometimes stress is just part of life. It is unavoidable, but it doesn't have to be unmanageable.

A key factor will always remain... which is that is when your blood sugar levels are balanced and your gut bacteria is in balance, your Zen world will become more and more available.

Action:

Where method meets lifestyle; the "Action" is the integration of a livable, maintainable and sustainable method. Unfortunately, life has productivity-hacks. It's important to analyze your life to create the most simplistic, streamlined plan of action.

Regardless of the method you choose, you will need a starting point. One thing each method will have in common is utilizing a "food journal" for every bite, every snack and meal. It's simple. It isn't subjective data. It's a fact. You only write it down if you consumed it. You might think you're eating well but upon review, you notice that you ate a cheeseburger, fries, soda and apple slices twice this week... yeah, that's not gonna cut it. The fact is, it's easy to forget the one piece of candy that became two or five or... You have to write it down and review it in a neutral state. Be sure to not only log what was consumed, but also note if you felt bloated, irritable, or maybe energetic and refreshed. This is a commitment and daily lifestyle assessment leading toward the optimal goal...CHANGE. You'll be able to zone in on your weakest areas. If you are a chocolate lover, then don't step into the candy store if it's not your treat day. If you have a glass of wine, then be prepared to work out for 40 minutes (1 hour for 2 glasses of wine). It is all about balance and a give and take.

From here forward make your action - reality to:

1. Avoid Marketing Gimmicks – keep your eye on the tiger

2. Journal your food, beverage, emotions and wins

3. Track weight, fat and sleep cycles

4. Have a system for hydration

5. If it comes in a bag or box, don't eat it

6. Eat whole foods such as: meat, fish, vegetable, fruits, nuts, seeds and starches like potatoes and sweet potatoes

7. Eat a cooked and a raw green vegetable every day

8. Drink green juice for a meal at least one meal per week

9. Choose local and organic produce whenever possible

10. Choose pasture-raised animal products and wild-caught fish whenever possible

11. Move, exercise, stretch, and try to get outdoors for your dose of Vitamin D

12. Prepare your body, mind and kitchen for a healthier and happier lifestyle

13. Implement sure-fire strategies to sustain the new habits you have created

14. Preparation is key… make up snacks ahead of time for the week

15. Create recipes ideas that are no-cook ideas to easily reference

16. If you have a crazy week ahead of you, make stew, soup or crock-pot meals

These methods and key points are your weapon of defense so you can live well. Food is not your adversary. It makes you beautiful and alive like the butterfly amongst the flower. Once you get some fundamental healthy regimes in a personalized system, you will be able to easily repeat them. You'll have the moment of, "Phew! I have finally found an eating lifestyle that I can follow forever!"

Living this will give you such vitality and hope. You will feel so good, almost invincible… Even though you may not be eating specific to your DNA, your body can feel rejuvenated simply by *living* with these healthy habits. Try it… you'll find it invigorating and addictive.

This lifestyle is not about forgetting all the foods you love and trading them in for a regimental diet that you must live and die by. This is where you say, "YES! I *will*, I *can* make these adaptations to my life and create a sustainable and INTENTIONAL way of living!" So WELCOME… welcome to LOVING the *life* you *live* IN and finding YOUR FOOD-TRUTH!

To contact Tamara:

Tamara Renee Global

Founder and Creator of, Tamara Renee LLC, DNA Diet Method and Club ME Experience

Direct: 858.864.9333

E: TR@TamaraRenee.com

W: TamaraRenee.com, ClubMeExperience.com

http://www.fbt1.com/tamara2/#1

http://www.TamaraReneeDNA.com

http://facebook.com/tamarareneeDNA2

The Change 2

AFTERWORD

Life is always a series of transitions…people, places and things that shape who we are as individuals. Often you never know that the next catalyst for change is around the corner.

Jim Britt and Jim Lutes have spent decades influencing individuals to blossom into the best version of themselves.

Allow all you have read in this book to create introspection and redirection if required. It's your journey to craft.

The Change is a series. Watch for future releases and add them to your collection. If you know of anyone who would like to be considered as a co-author for a future book have them email our offices at support@jimbritt.com

The individual and combined works of Jim Britt and Jim Lutes have filled seminar rooms to maximum capacity and created a worldwide demand.

The blessings go both ways as Jim and Jim are always willing students of life. Out of demand for life changing programs and events Jim and Jim conduct seminars worldwide as well as created a global company in over 170 countries called Quanta International, that allows anyone to benefit behaviorally as well as financially.

If you would like to hear more about how the Quanta company can assist you in both income generating and personal development please email our offices at: quanta@jimbritt.com

To Schedule Jim Britt or Jim Lutes as your featured speaker and your next convention or special event email: support@JimBritt.com

Master your moment as they become hours that become days.

Your legacy awaits.

Blessings

Jim Britt and Jim Lutes

www.ingramcontent.com/pod-product-compliance
Lightning Source LLC
Chambersburg PA
CBHW071900290426
44110CB00013B/1223